Musée National Picasso – Paris

Anne Baldassari
Head curator
Curator of the opening exhibition
of the museum's collection

PICASSO
MuséePicassoParis
Flammarion

1895
1905

"For me painting is a dramatic action in the course of which reality finds itself split apart."

Pablo Picasso, in Robert Desnos, *Écrits sur les peintres* (Paris: Flammarion, 1984)

In 1895, and at only fourteen years of age, Pablo Picasso painted his first important oils on canvas: *La Fillette aux pieds nus* (*The Barefoot Girl*) and *L'Homme à la casquette* (*Man with a Cap*). At the time he was a student at the School of Fine Arts in La Coruña, where his father, José Ruiz Blasco, himself a painter, art restorer, and occasional museum curator, was a teacher.

Picasso would keep these two paintings with him for the rest of his life as testimony to these formative years. The young artist was then influenced both by the Spanish masters, such as Murillo, Velázquez, and Goya, and by minor artists from regional schools who decorated churches and monuments, and whose works he saw reproduced in illustrated magazines. As Picasso liked to point out, he never expressed himself like a child, even when young. Brought up to draw and paint "like Raphael," in fact he had to strive to unlearn the reflexes that academic training had instilled in him in order to forge the tools necessary for his own self-expression.

Representing Spain at the Exposition Universelle in 1900, with a picture titled *Science and Charity* (1896), Picasso discovered Paris and its nightlife. He visited the art galleries where paintings by Van Gogh, Gauguin, and Cézanne transformed his whole conception of painting. On the boulevards, the posters of Toulouse-Lautrec, Bonnard, and Steinlen converted him to the idea of the need for an art for the street. The great art dealer Ambroise Vollard devoted a first exhibition to him in summer 1901. The immediate success of such a young painter, giddy with society life, led him to a style with sumptuous colors but still steeped in convention. The art critic, Gustave Coquiot, defended his art and gave him a number of commissions, including the project for a poster for his play, *Théâtre Molière Sainte Roulette* (*Molière Sainte Roulette Theater*, 1904), an exceptional example of his work as a poster artist. The 1900–1901 period, polychromatic and expressionist in its intent, culminated in *La Mort de Casagemas* (*The Death of Casagemas*, 1901), which is testament to the significant influence of Vincent Van Gogh on Picasso's early work. In just a few months, the young prodigy was literally transformed by the paintings of the modernist masters.

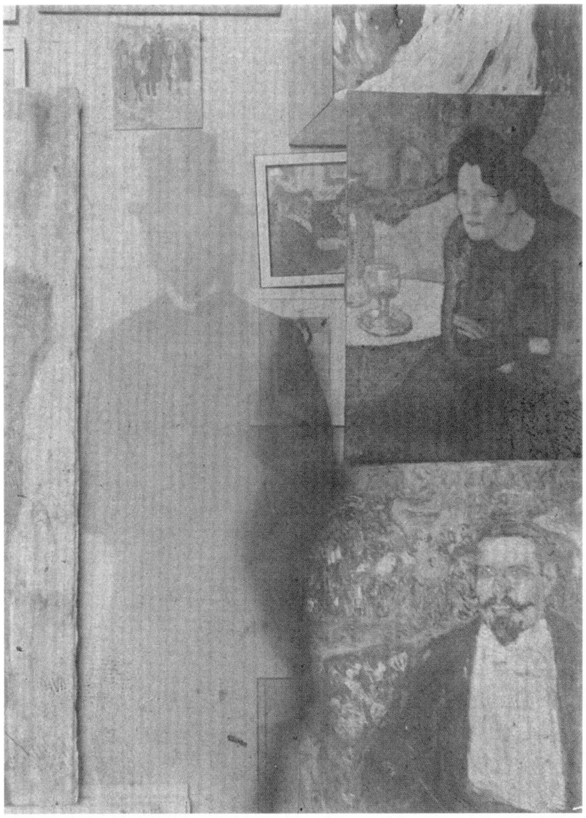

Self-portrait in the studio, [1901–2]

With emblematic figures of forlornness, *Autoportrait* (*Self-portrait*, 1901) and the *Portrait d'homme* (*Portrait of a Man*, 1902–3) seemed to transport the stiff figure of *L'Homme à la casquette* into the monochrome realm of the Blue Period. The similarities between the bearded faces, staring eyes, and constricted torsos, all painted to the same scale, are indeed striking. The tension across the canvases, however, exemplifies the aesthetic and ethical changes underway in Picasso's output. For Picasso, rather than a mere artifice of color—a signature—monochromaticity constituted both a chromatic "manifesto" that he shared with the principles of modernism, and a plastic means of unifying the space of the motif with the background, a strategy that predates and prefigures the synthesis that the cubist revolution would soon achieve.

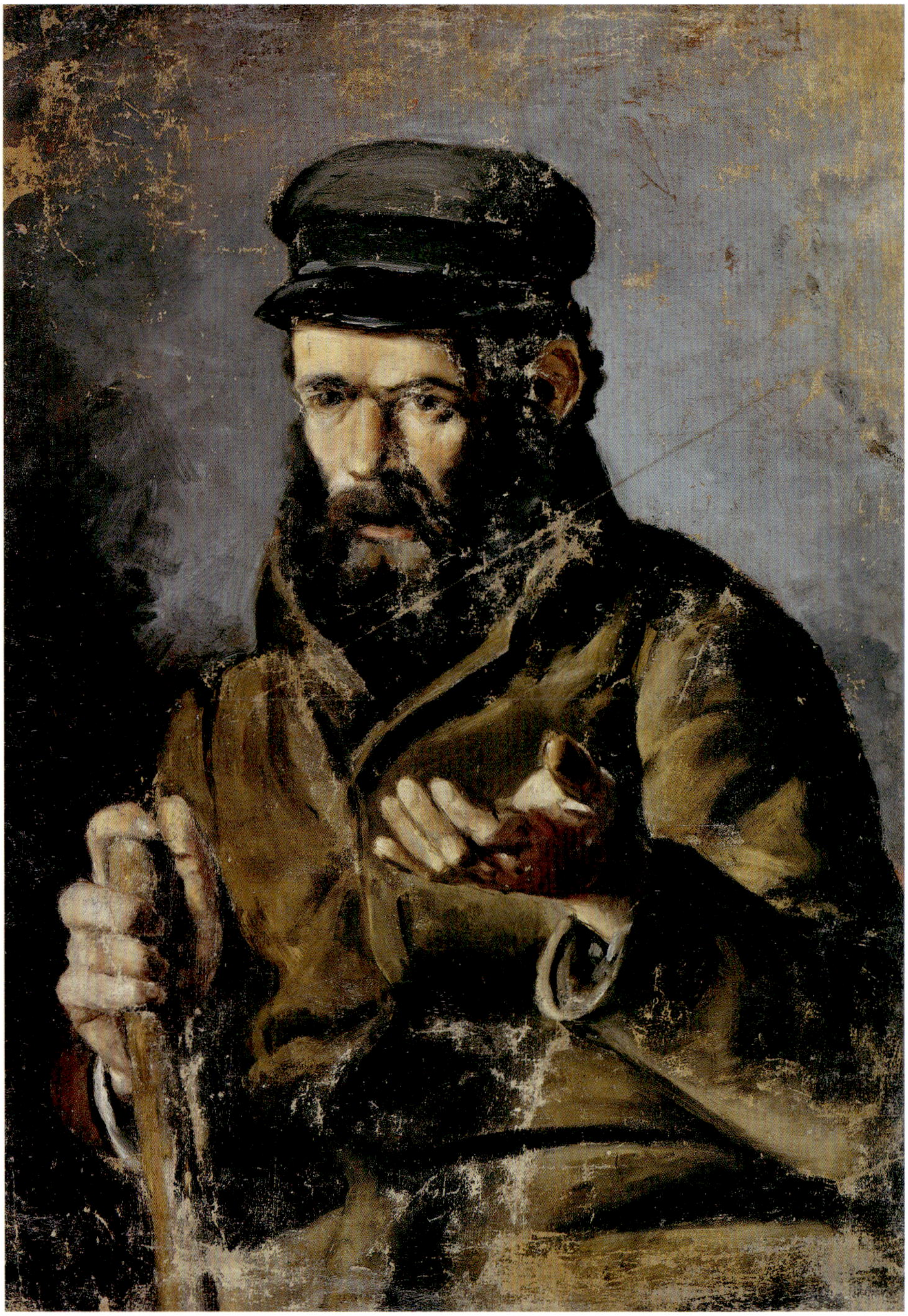

4 *Man with a Cap*, early 1895

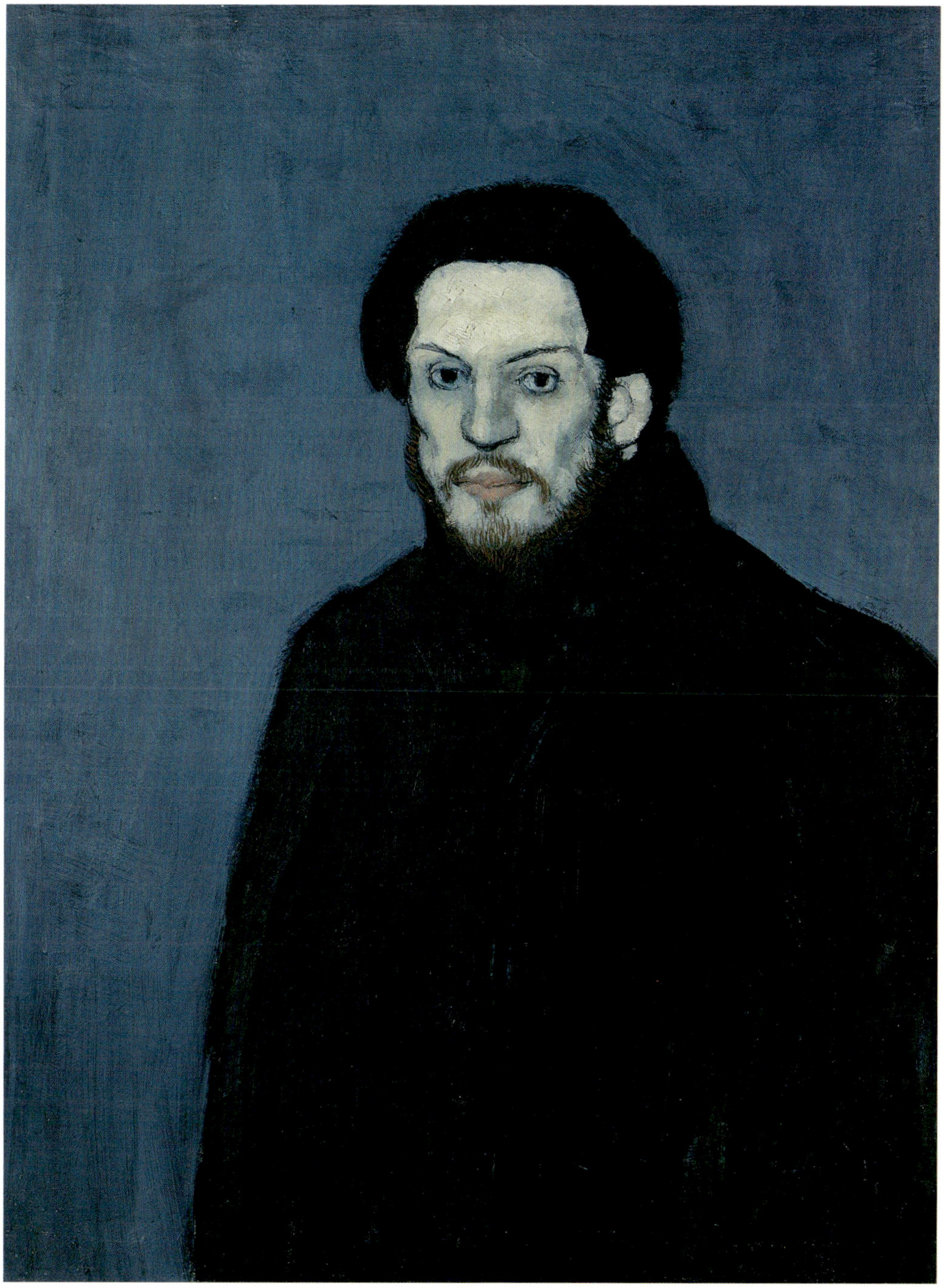

Self-portrait, late 1901

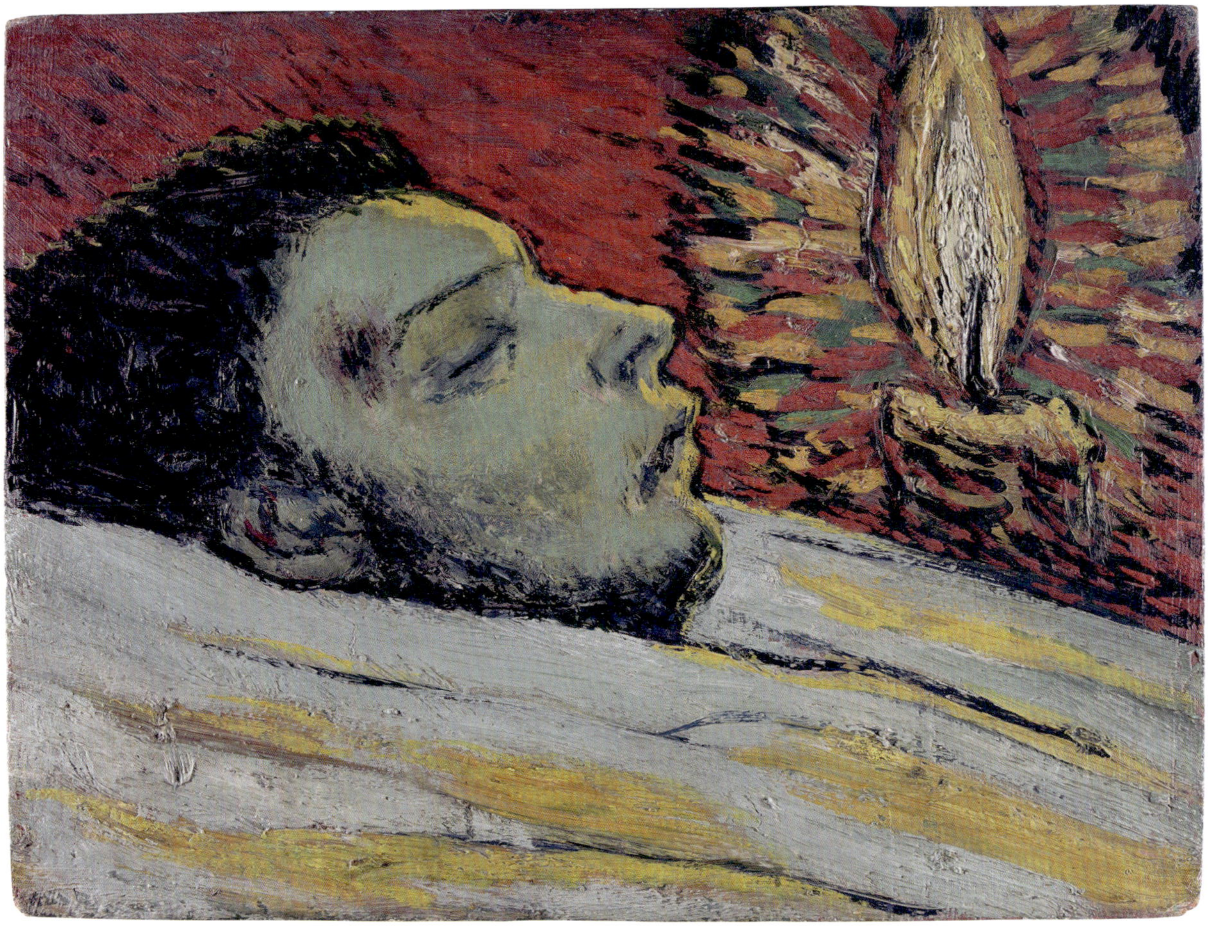

6 *The Death of Casagemas*, summer 1901

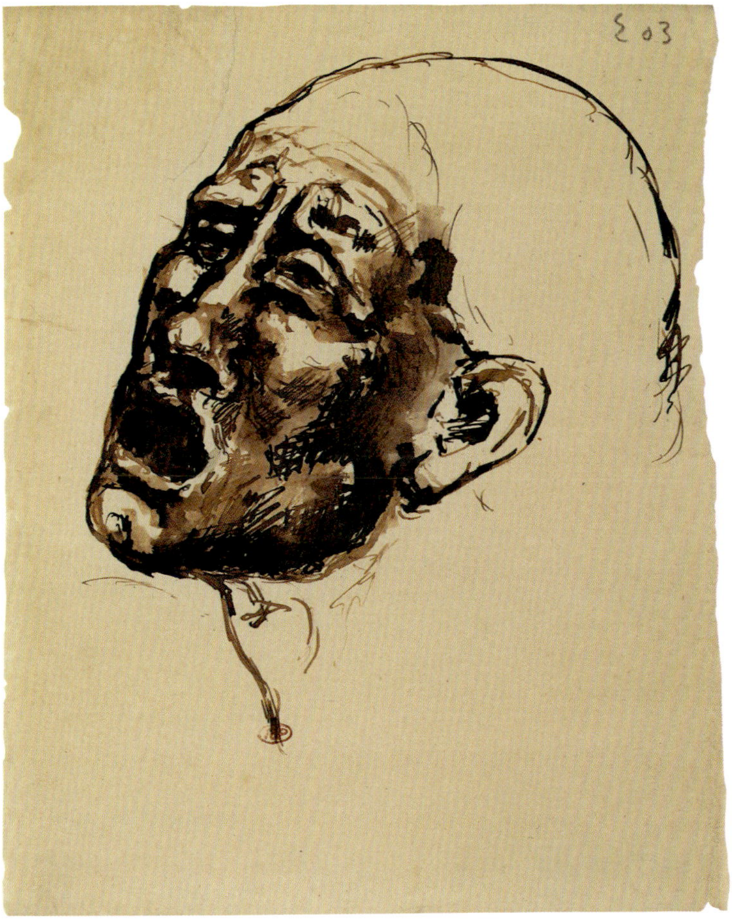

Head of Crying Woman, January 1903

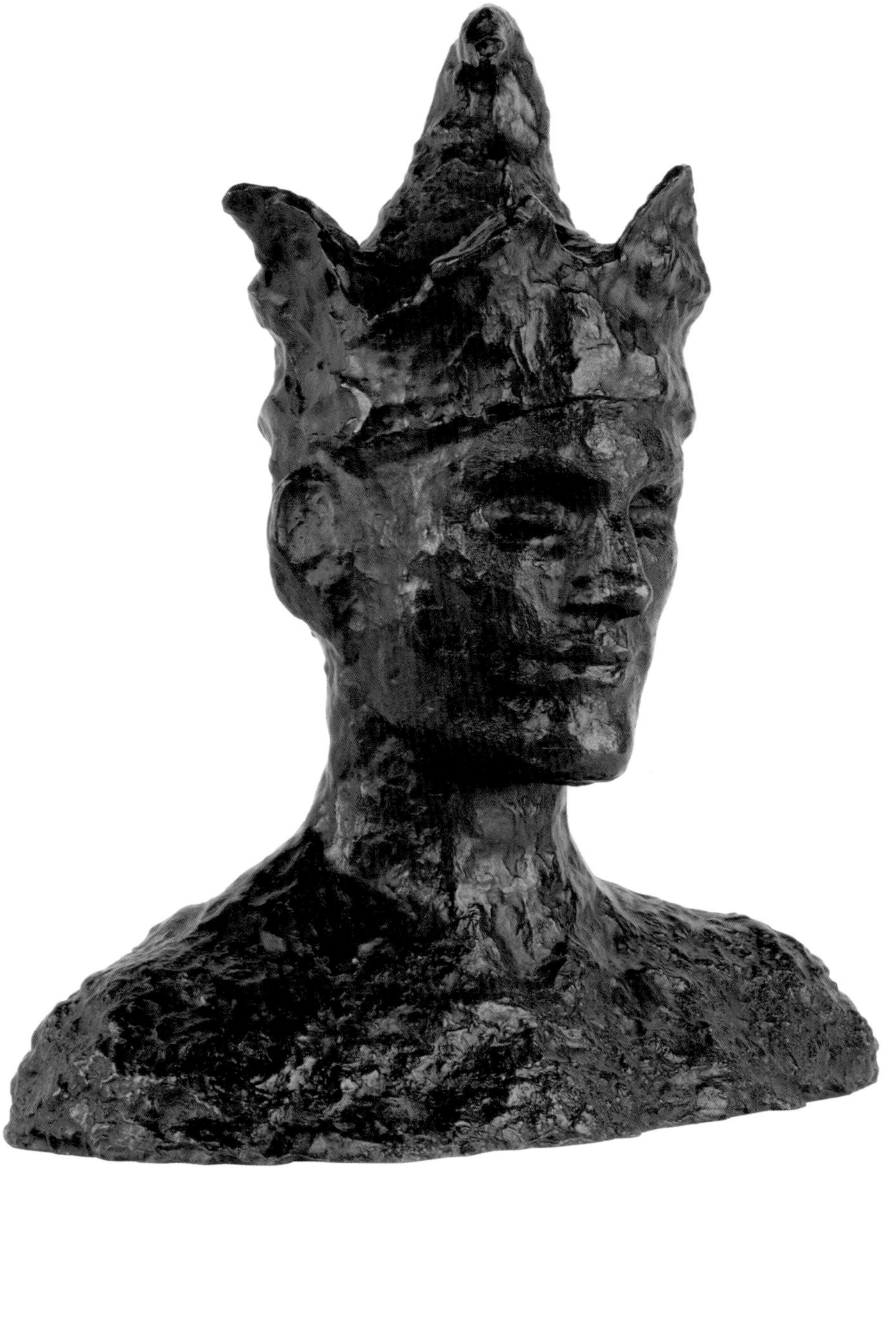

8 *The Jester*, 1905

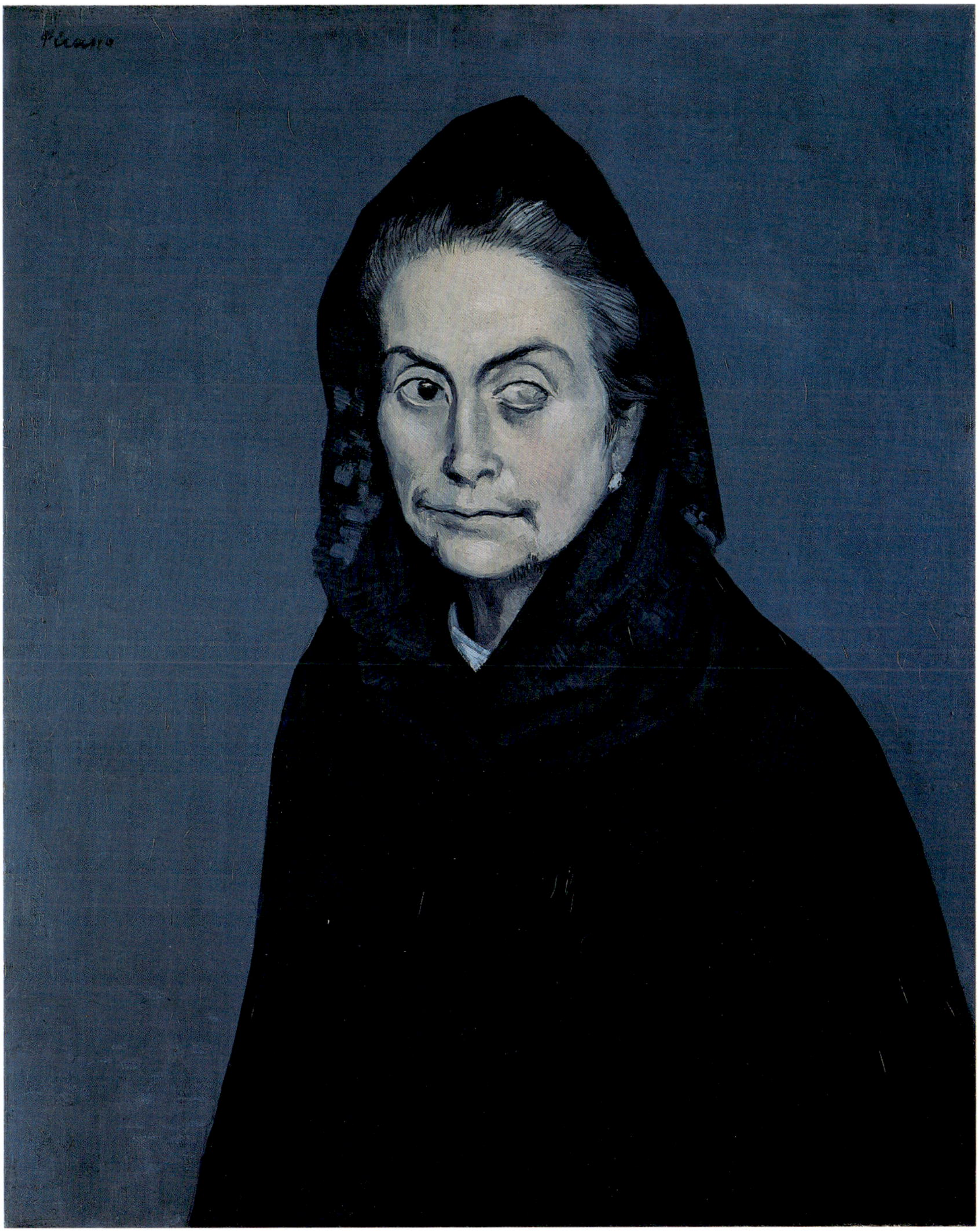

La Célestine, March 1904

1906
1909

"I kept on looking at the fetishes.
Then I understood that
I myself am also against everything."

Pablo Picasso, in André Malraux, *Picasso's Mask* (New York: Da Capo Press, 1995), originally published in French as *La Tête d'obsidienne* (Paris: Gallimard, 1974)

From spring 1906, the pinks of the Rose Period veered more toward ocher, with Picasso borrowing themes, perceptive foreshortenings, and a primitivist expressivity from Gauguin. At the time of the trip to Gósol during the summer, such references, together with an interest in Iberian art and Catalan Romanesque sculpture, led Picasso to abrupt simplifications of form and space. The bronzes *Femme se coiffant* (*Woman Dressing Her Hair*) and *Tête de femme* (*Fernande*) (*Head of a Woman* [*Fernande*]), are similar to the pink *Autoportrait* (*Self-portrait*), in which the painter portrays himself naked, and demonstrated the importance in 1906 of Gauguin as a source in the construction of this new formal vocabulary. From this moment on, moreover, the experimental relation between painting, sculpture, and engraving played a crucial role in the "laboratory" of Picasso's oeuvre.

During winter 1906–7, Picasso produced a vast amount of drawing centered on the project for *Les Demoiselles d'Avignon* (Museum of Modern Art, New York). The many sketchbooks preserved in the Musée Picasso show how the theme and its treatment evolved over time. To further his analysis and his quest for simplified forms, the artist used ethnographic photos and postcards of "indigenous African types." He also acquired two carved heads from the Iberian period, producing a group of paintings presenting details from, or cutouts of, his great composition. Like the heads and the giant caryatids from the front or the rear, *Nu assis* (*Seated Nude*) disposes each sign so as to "name" in an unprecedented language the eye, ear, mouth, chest, and hands of this new type of female physique invented in painting. *Seated Nude* (1906–7), *Femme nue de trois quarts dos* (*Nude Woman, Three-Quarters Back View*, 1907), and *Femme aux mains jointes* (*Woman with Clasped Hands*, 1907), provide evidence of the process of architectonic deconstruction on which Picasso embarked from winter 1906 to spring 1907. The figures, whose primitivism had already integrated Cézanne's approach in terms of the geometrization of volumes, understood as "treating nature by the cylinder, the sphere, the cone, with the whole in perspective" (Cézanne, letter to Émile Bernard, April 15, 1904), free themselves from the illusionist procedure of portraying reality. The procedure behind this radicalization is evident in a large wood carving of 1907, engraved and with touches of color, titled *Figure*. The first, "Iberian" or "Rose" state of *Les Demoiselles d'Avignon* was probably completed by March/April. As Apollinaire records: "Seen his new painting: uniform colors, flesh pinks, flowers, etc., similar and simplified women's heads, men's heads too. Admirable language that no literature can compete with, because our words all already exist. Alas!" (*Journal intime*, 1907). His studies of the African and Oceanic tribal art in the collections of the Musée d'Art et d'Ethnographie du Trocadéro, undertaken from summer 1907, remain central to our understanding of the development of his work at this time. Following his visit to the Trocadéro, Picasso repainted the right-hand section of the composition before the end of July in a radical stylistic idiom. The picture's innovative zest, its self-evident ambition to foment a visual revolution, aroused astonishment, consternation even, among the artist's immediate circle. Georges Braque declared to Daniel-Henry Kahnweiler: "*Les Demoiselles d'Avignon*? It was as if somebody drank oil so as to spit out fire." André Derain worried about "finding Picasso one day hanged behind his large picture." As for Félix Fénéon, he considered the work "incomprehensible," and advised the artist to devote his efforts henceforth to caricature. For Henri Matisse and Leo Stein, both spellbound, the picture had passed through to the other side of the "fourth dimension." André Salmon, a friend, concludes this incredulous critical outburst: "A little forsaken, Picasso found himself in the company of African omens... and dashed off several frightening nudes, grimacing and perfectly deserving of our loathing."

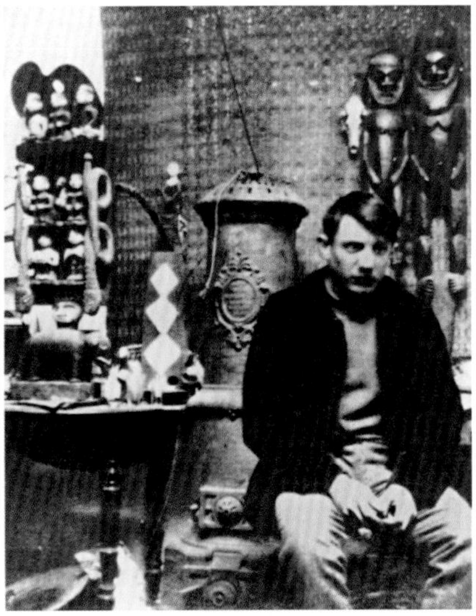

Picasso in the studio at the Bateau-Lavoir, 1908,
by Frank Gelett Burgess

During the period 1907–8, Picasso carried out the "great tableau" of *Trois femmes* (*Three Women*, State Hermitage Museum, St. Petersburg), a work preceded by many studies held by the museum. This recurring motif features in the important canvas, *Trois figures sous un arbre* (*Three Figures under a Tree*), which is typical of the "African" period in that it includes figures to which architectural rigor and chromatic reduction confer singular formal power. The painting is as if tattooed on the androgynous scaffolding of the bodies in it. In this "cosmogonic" era, which saw the foundation of a new universe of artistic meaning, the painter populated his canvases with mythological creatures, such as nymphs and the Graces, forming schema of ternary allegory.

Condensing the research undertaken in the summer in Horta de Ebro, in *Head of a Woman* (*Fernande*) (1909), the scarification of the pictorial surface is extended to sculpture. Picasso gouges into the volume until the head is almost pierced through; bristling with razor-sharp edges and wounds, and shorn of the influences of Auguste Rodin and Medardo Rosso. These constituted the earliest experiments with "open" volume, anticipating the perforated sculptures of the *Guitars* and the *Violins* of 1912–15.

During summer 1909, retreating to Horta de Ebro and in the solitude of the mountains, the fundamental principles underpinning Picasso's cubism attained greater definition. The task involved the methodical deconstruction of reality by means of photography, a medium used by Picasso since the beginning of the century to document his work in the studio. He subsequently used it for recording landscapes and for "taking portraits" of local farmers. In the pictures painted in Horta, a fusion of composite views between various photos taken in the village combines into a convex space and a representation of volume in reversed perspective. Such characteristics reactivated the rules of icon painting of the Byzantine tradition, to which the artist added references to El Greco, Robert Campin, and Van der Weyden, interweaving them with discoveries made during experiments with stereoscopy and negative overprinting. Generating uncertain reliefs, optical foreshortenings, veiled, duplicated, multiplied images, this hybrid research did much to model the optical "braiding" of the surface that is characteristic of Picasso's brand of cubism.

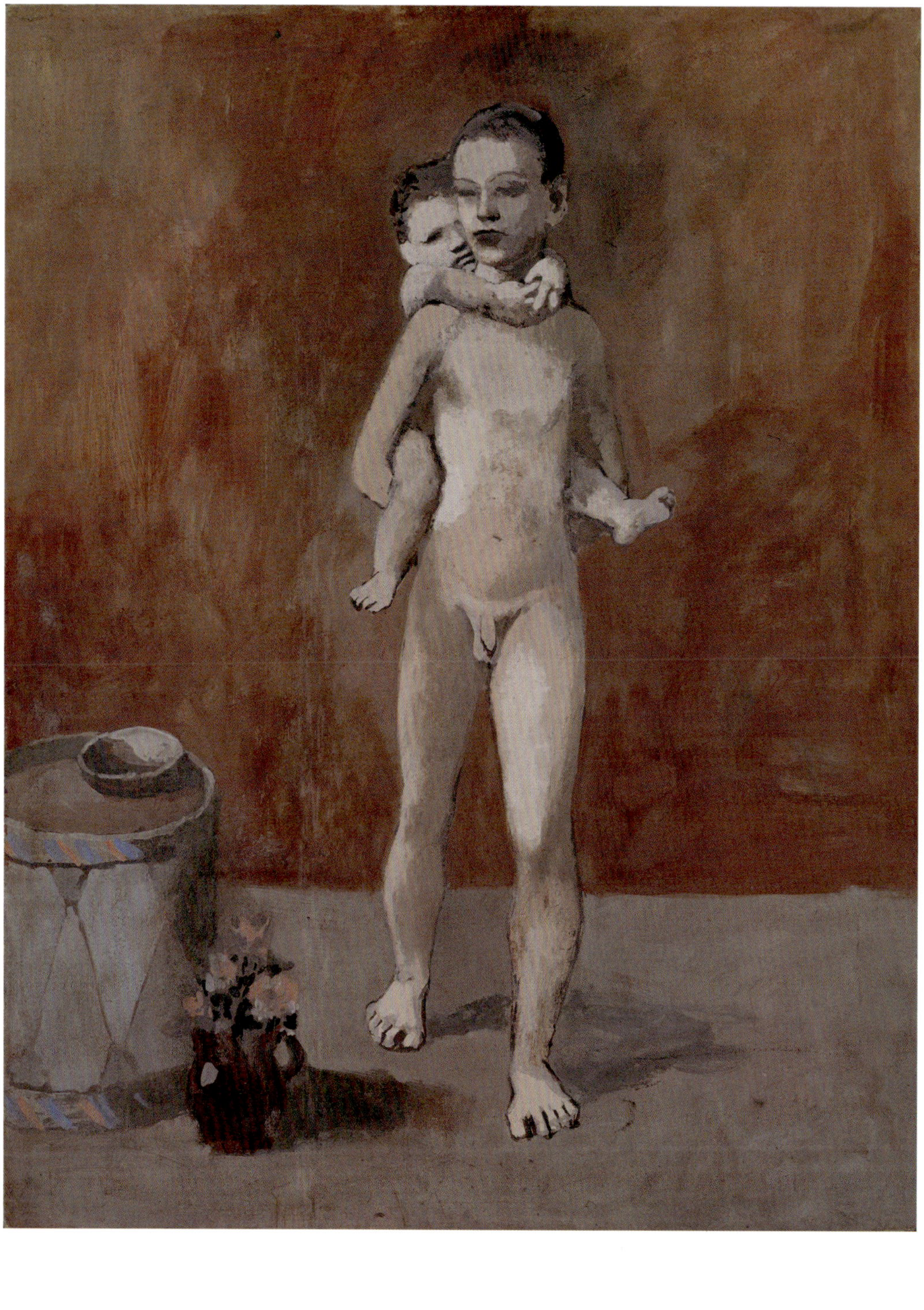

12 *The Two Brothers*, summer 1906

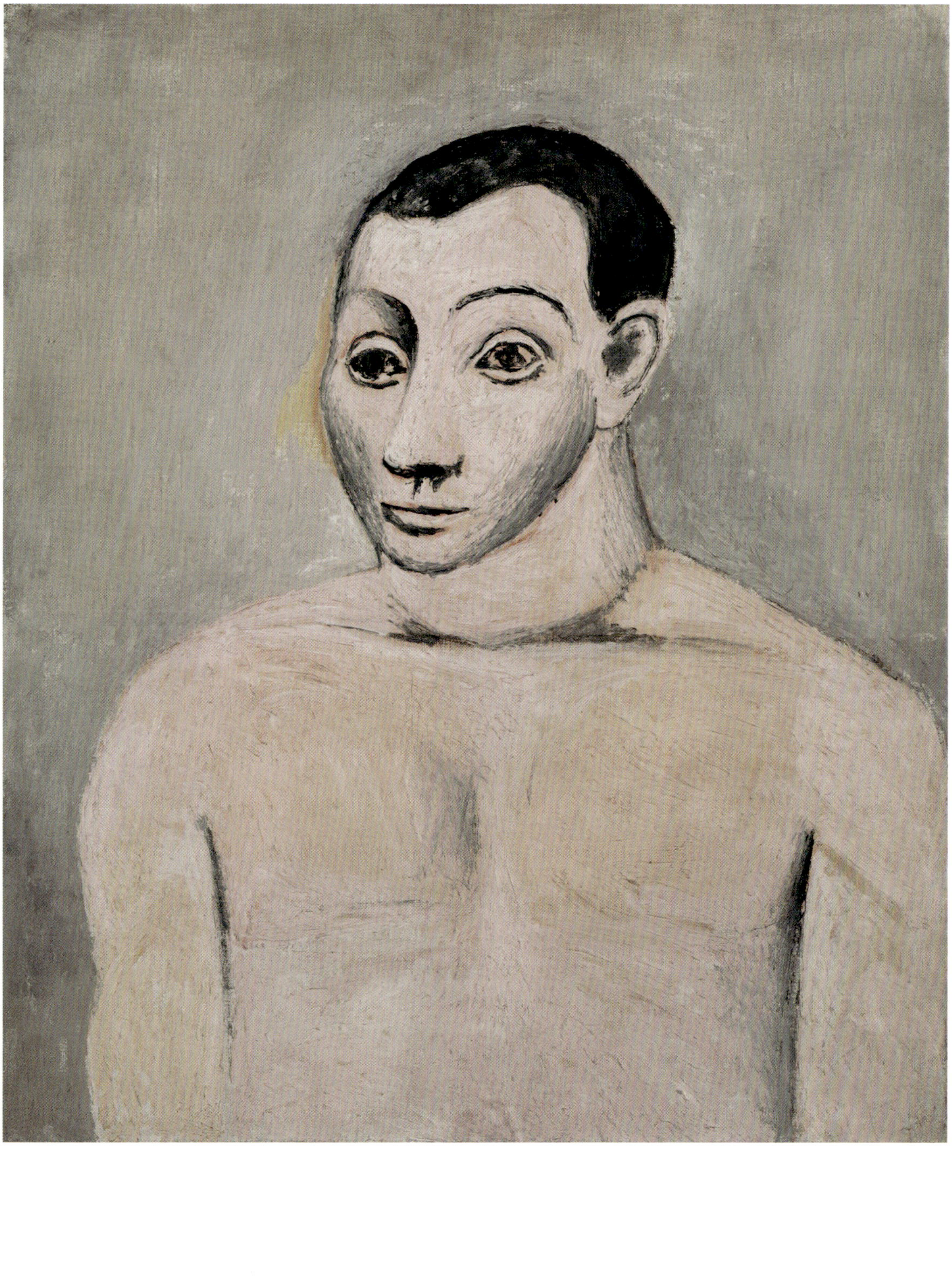

Self-portrait, fall 1906

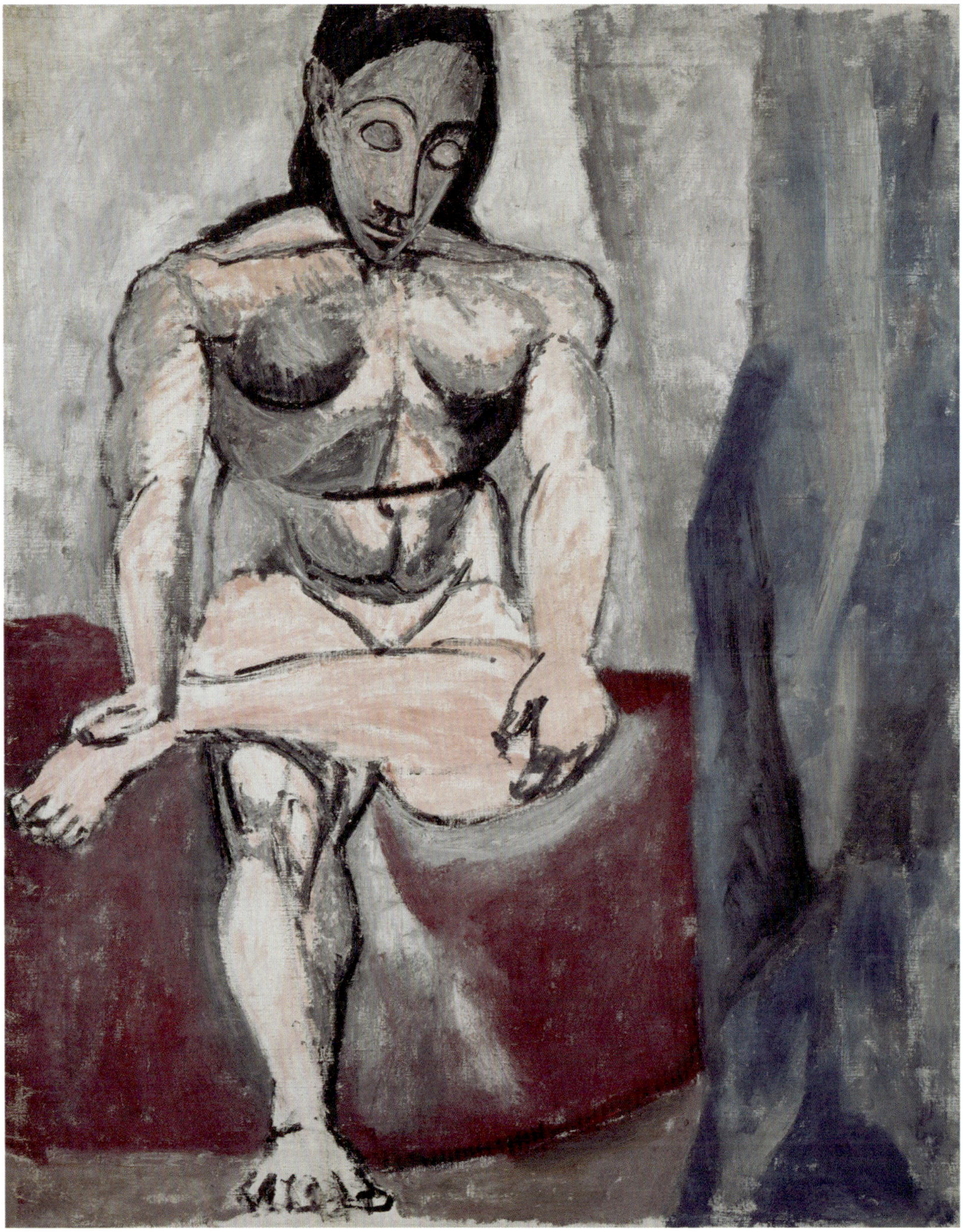

14 *Seated Nude* (Study for *Les Demoiselles d'Avignon*), winter 1906–7

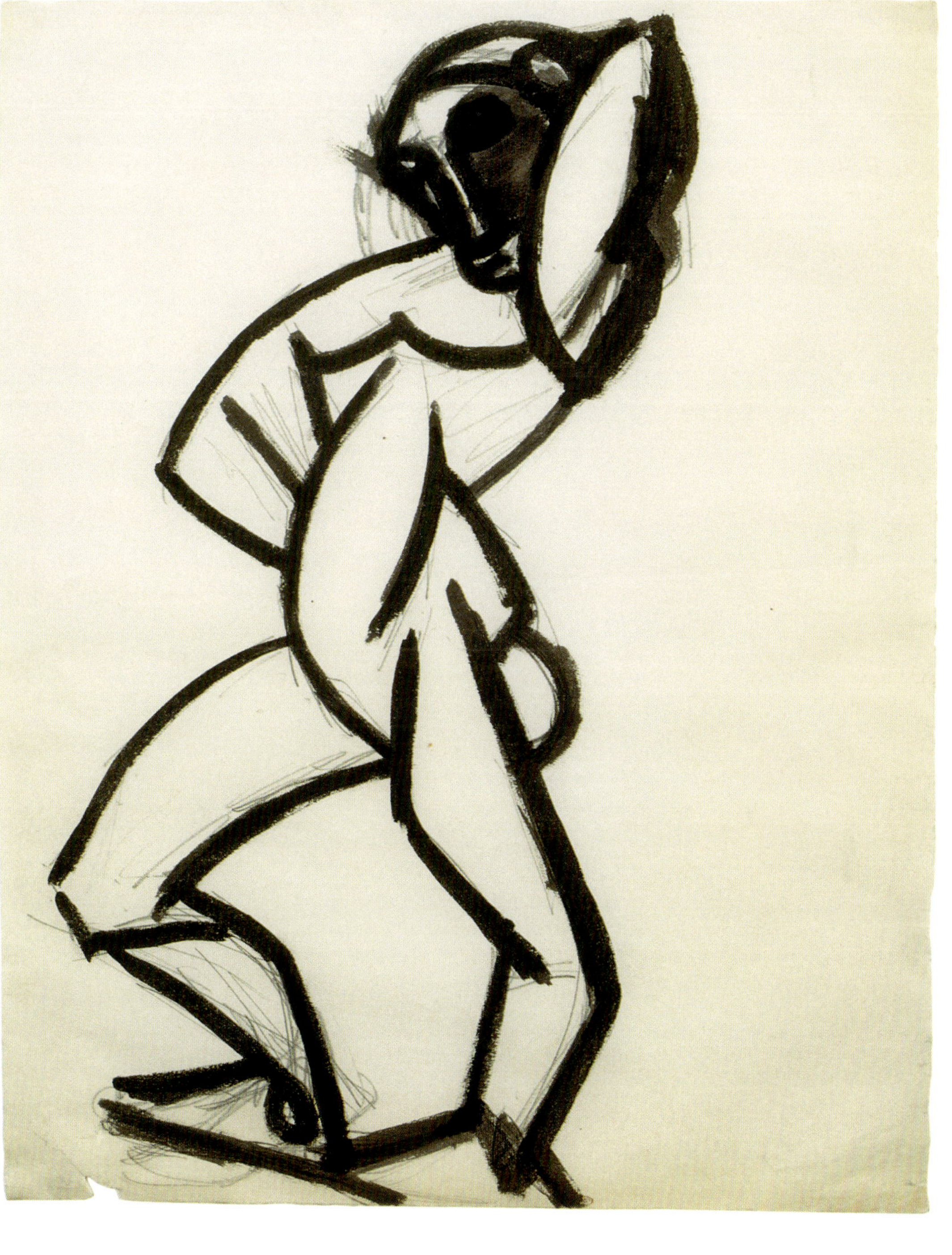

Nude with Raised Arm, spring 1908

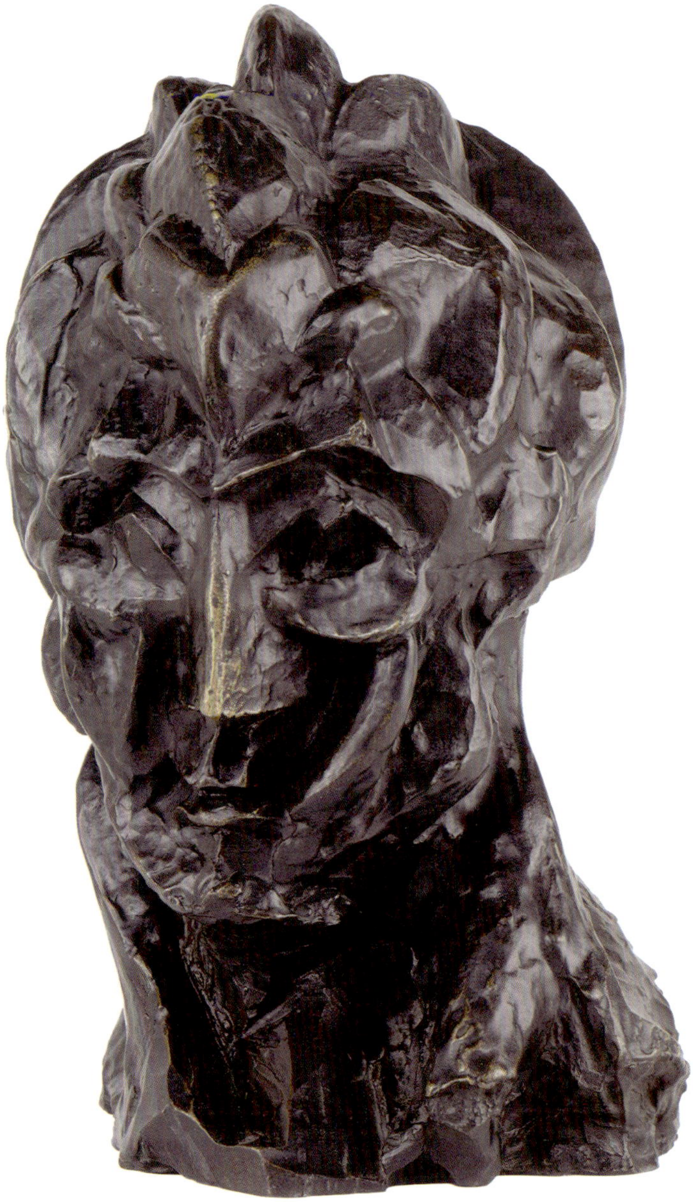

16 *Head of a Woman (Fernande)*, fall 1909

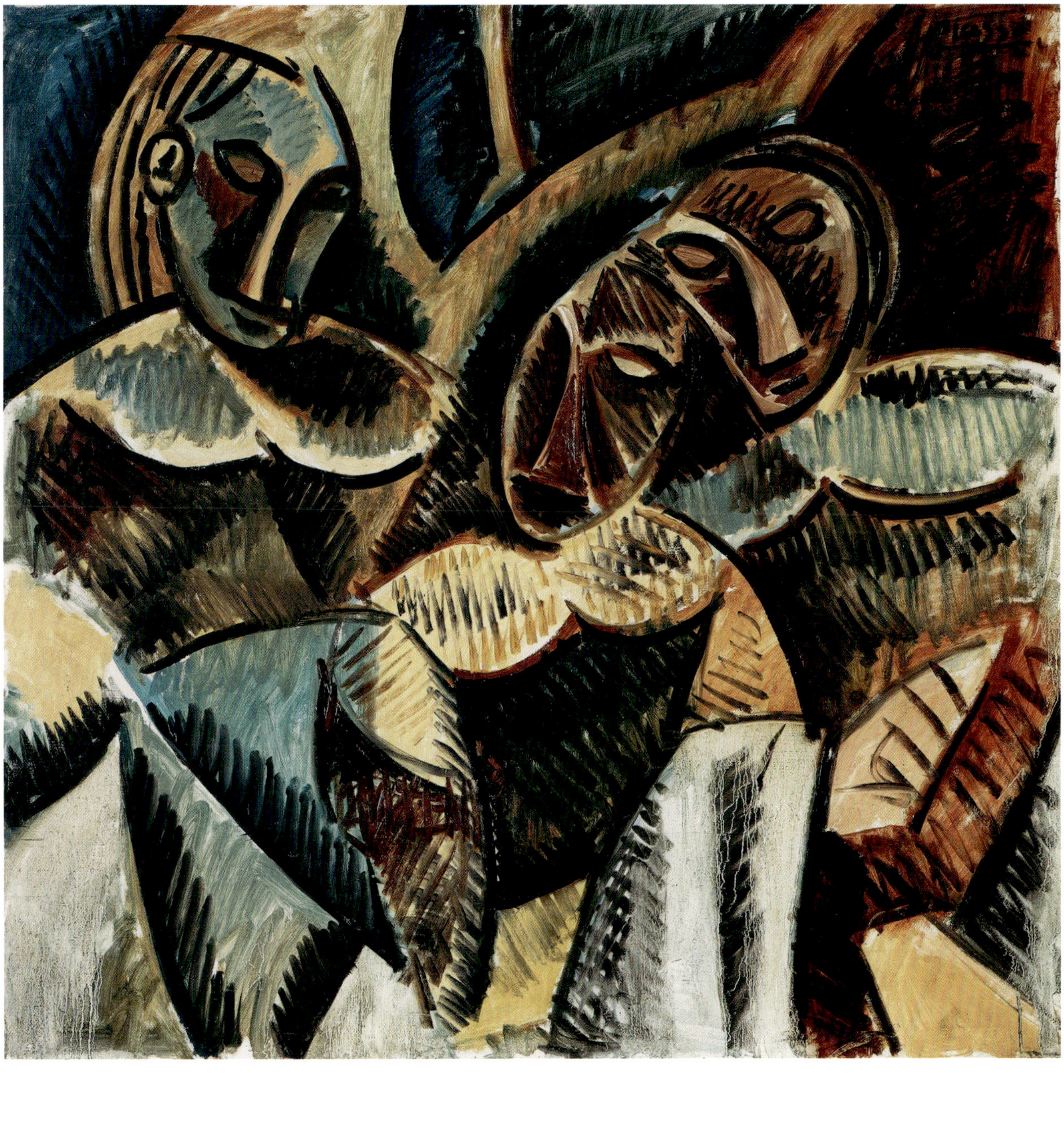

Three Figures under a Tree, winter 1907–8

1910
1915

"Art should not be
a *trompe-l'oeil*,
but a *trompe-l'esprit*."

Pablo Picasso, in Robert Desnos, *Écrits sur les peintres* (Paris: Flammarion, 1984)

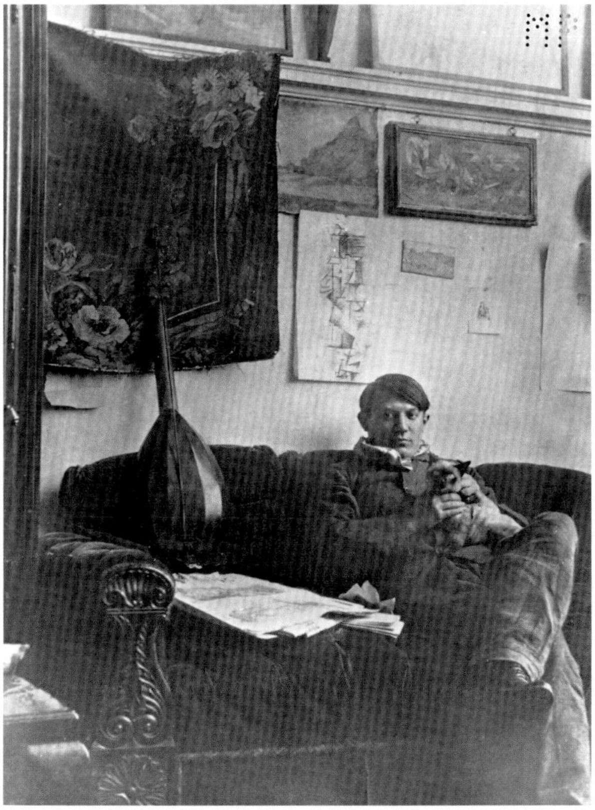
Self-portrait in the studio on boulevard de Clichy, 1910

From 1910, Picasso endeavored not to portray the optical appearance of the world, but to transfer the complexity of a potential reality onto the picture plane: "One of the fundamental tenets of cubism was to shift reality; reality was no longer in the object, it was in the painting." (Françoise Gilot and Carlton Lake, *Life with Picasso*, 1964). The artist exposes a figure, an object, like a plan for assembling specific perceptions: simplified volumes that open up along an edge; division of the surface into successive planes; transparency of the planes; foregrounding and schematization of internal structure; decomposition of the volume into facets.

In 1912, with *Nature morte à la chaise cannée* (*Still Life with Cane Chair*), a composite piece combining trompe l'oeil printed on waxed industrial canvas, painting, and string, Picasso created the first collage in modern art. Wallpaper, fabric, letterpress: the most sundry objects insinuate themselves into compositions and constructions from 1914, such as *Guitare et bouteille de Bass* (*Guitar and Bottle of Bass*) from 1913, *Verre, bouteille de vin, paquet de tabac, journal* (*Glass, Bottle of Wine, Packet of Tobacco, and Newspaper*), and *Verre, pipe, as de trèfle et dé* (*Glass, Pipe, Ace of Clubs, and Die*), works that experiment with space and usher in the third dimension, short-circuiting our perceptions. There is no longer "representation" in the work, but "presentation." In these canvases, constructions, drawings, and papiers collés, his poetic intention is to associate, in the manner of Stéphane Mallarmé's visual and typographical signs, puns, and *calligrammes*.

Centered on the diptych of the panels *Homme à la mandoline* (*Man with a Mandolin*, 1911) and *Homme à la guitare* (*Man with a Guitar*, 1911), the collection includes a succession of generic paintings in which the decomposition of form attains a high level of abstraction. These monochrome panels—black and white, or grisaille, in Indian ink and wash—play a didactic role that once again affirmed the new aesthetic principles of cubism. The term "hermetic cubism" would be applied to these works, whose schematic character made Picasso observe: "Cubist painters, amazed at their own work, began to erect a scaffolding of theories to justify them. Cubism, however, never possessed a program. A picture can represent the idea of things; it can, in addition, represent the appearance of things, without jeopardizing them." (*Lettre sur l'art*, 1926). André Breton, the founder of surrealism, admired the "scaffolding" in these canvases, whose "rigid frame" seemed to him to be buffeted by "high winds." The subversive lyricism of these "haunted" paintings revolutionized the codes of figuration "from top to bottom." (*Le Surréalisme et la peinture*, 1928).

To construct the cubist language, Picasso relied on what he dubbed "attributes" to inform the composition. These direct references to the usual forms of representation—illusionist facsimile, details, trompe l'oeil, copies, and pastiches—are encrypted, not only to ensure figural continuity, but also to intensify the visual dynamic. From 1914, the resurgence of such references accelerated, in particular through the use of popular imagery (postcards, advertisements, chromolithographs, etc.). *Le Peintre et son modèle* (*The Painter and His Model*) is regarded as the first act in this explicit "return" of the image. This modest canvas, between drawing and painting, line and color, establishes a link between cubist codification and figuration. Crudely labeled as a "return to order" by orthodox critics, the artist's elaborate undertaking enabled the development of a new phase of cubism—ironic, ambiguous, and subversive.

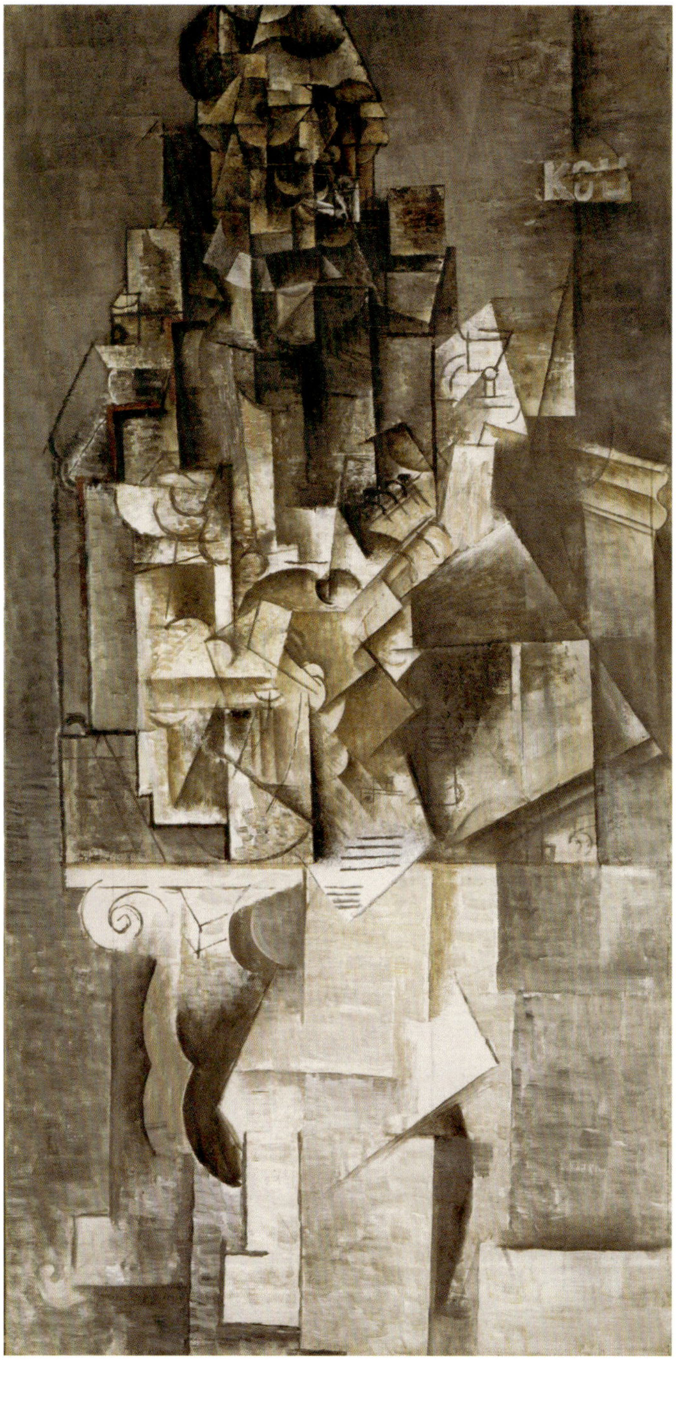

 Man with a Guitar, fall 1911–13

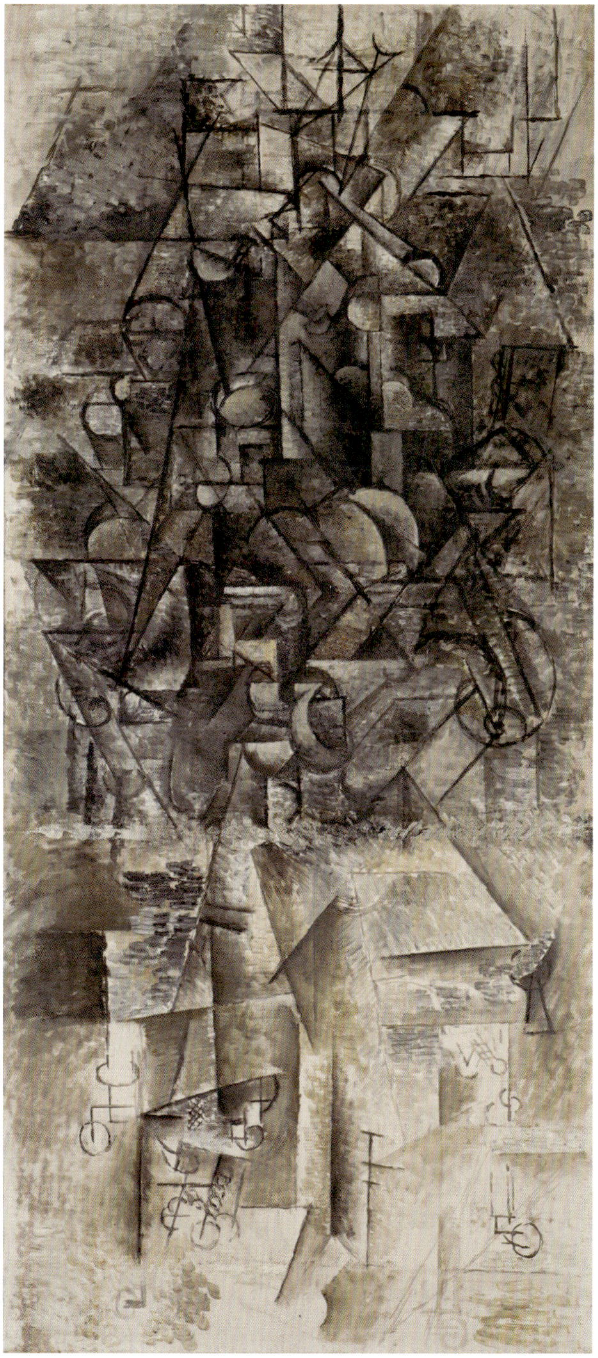

Man with a Mandolin, fall 1911

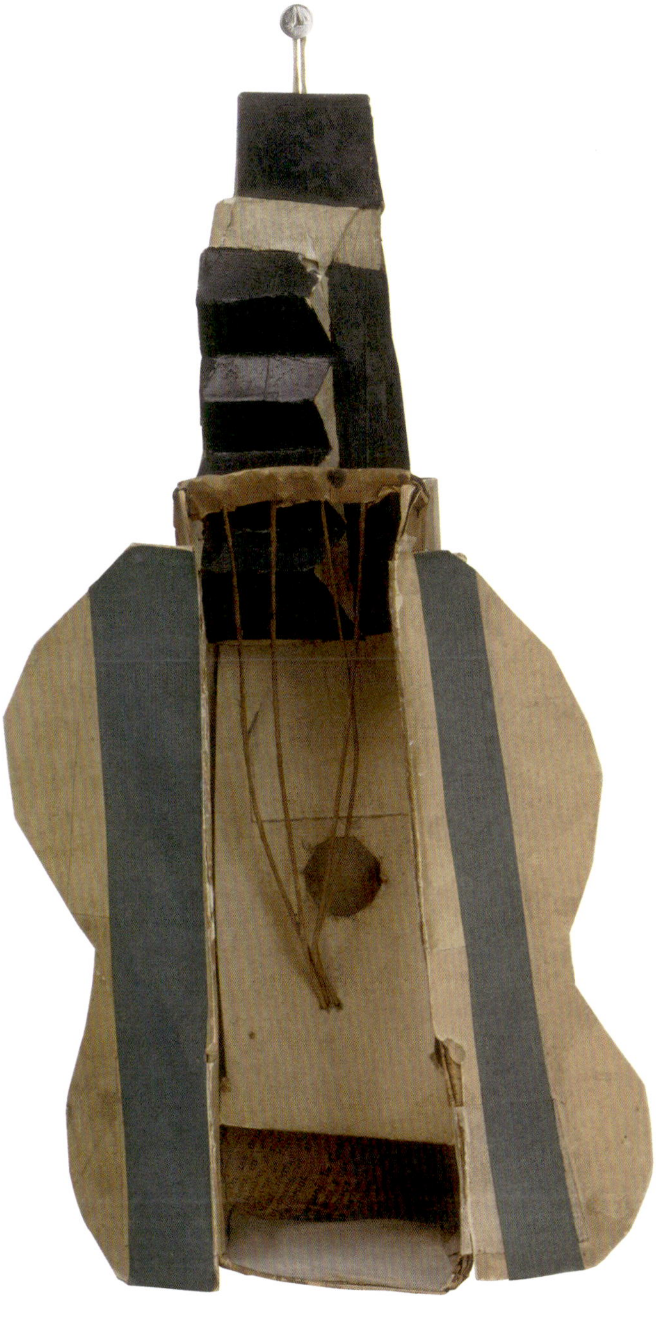

22 *Guitar*, December 1912

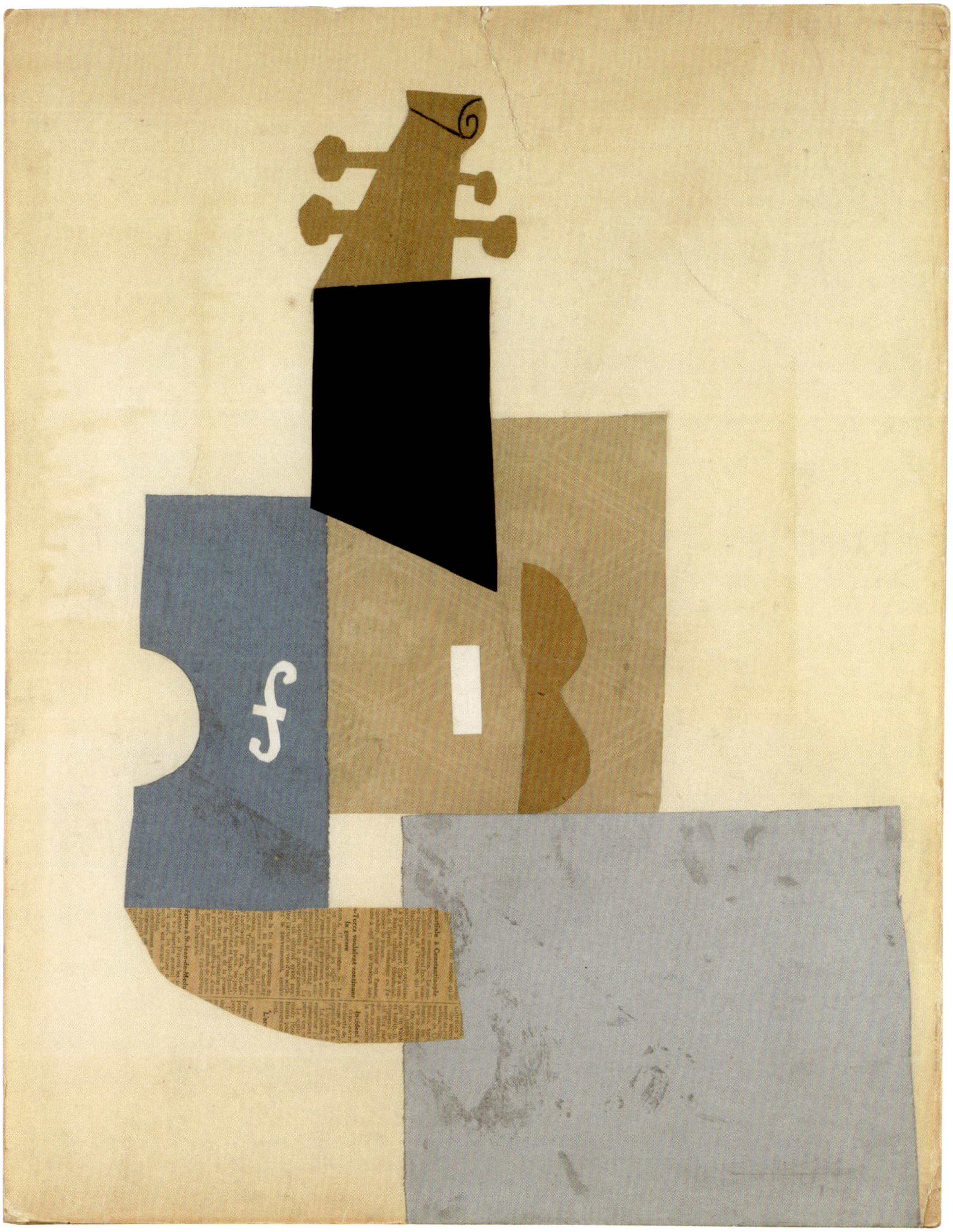

Violin, December 1913

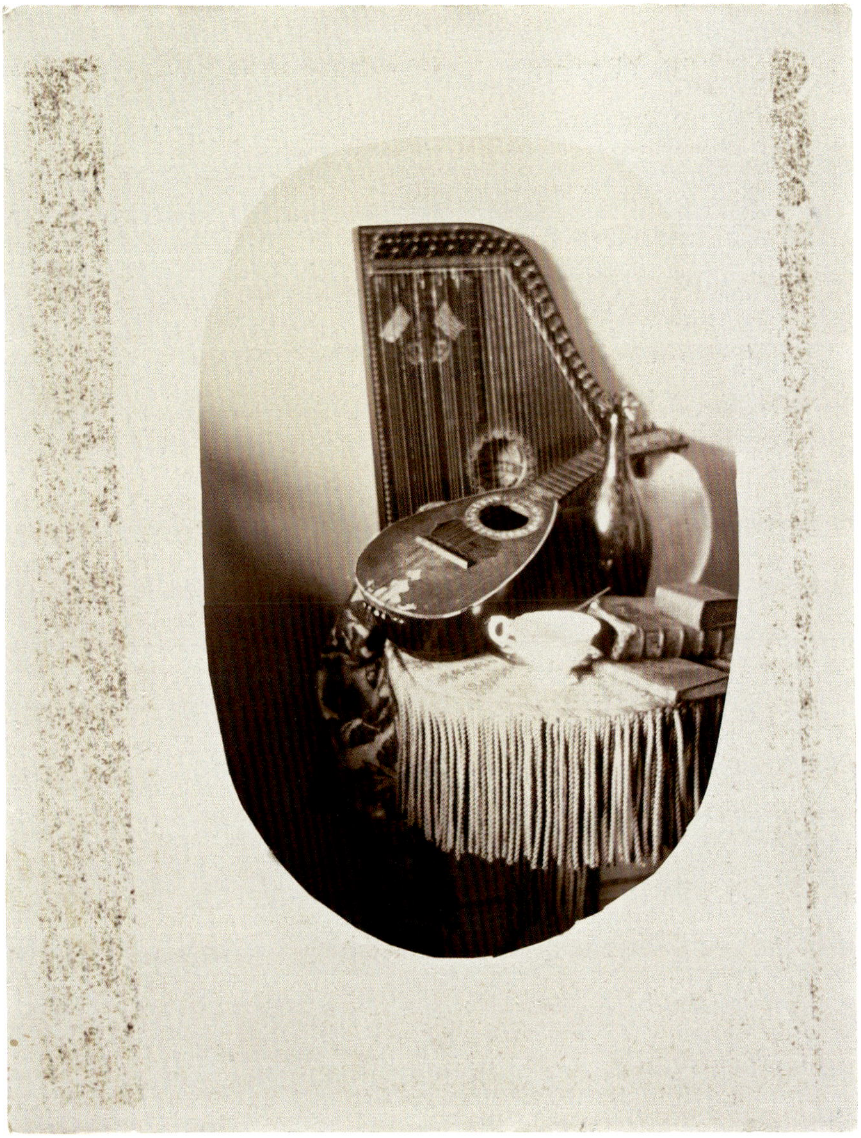

 Composition for Still Life on a Pedestal, 1911

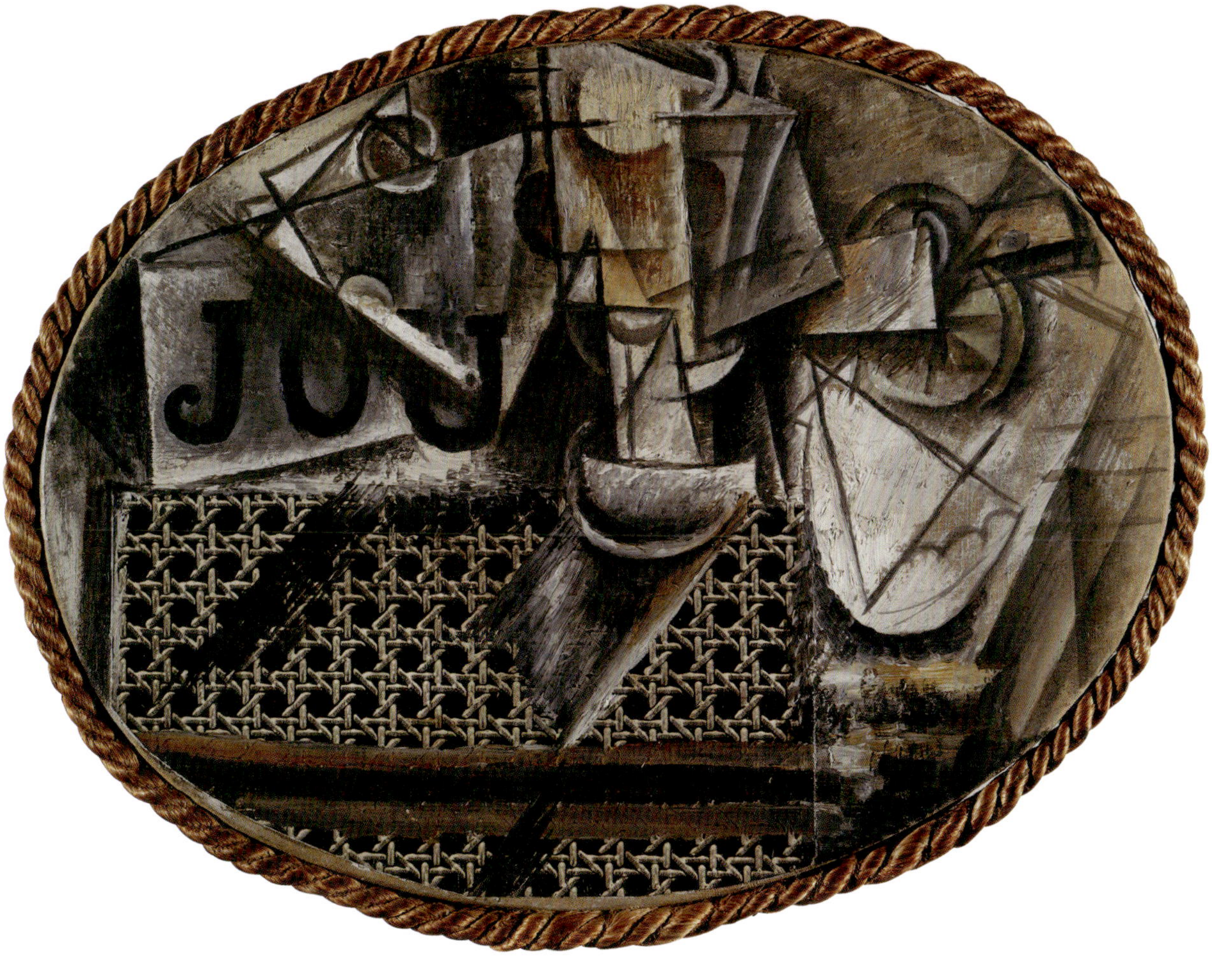

Still Life with Cane Chair, spring 1912

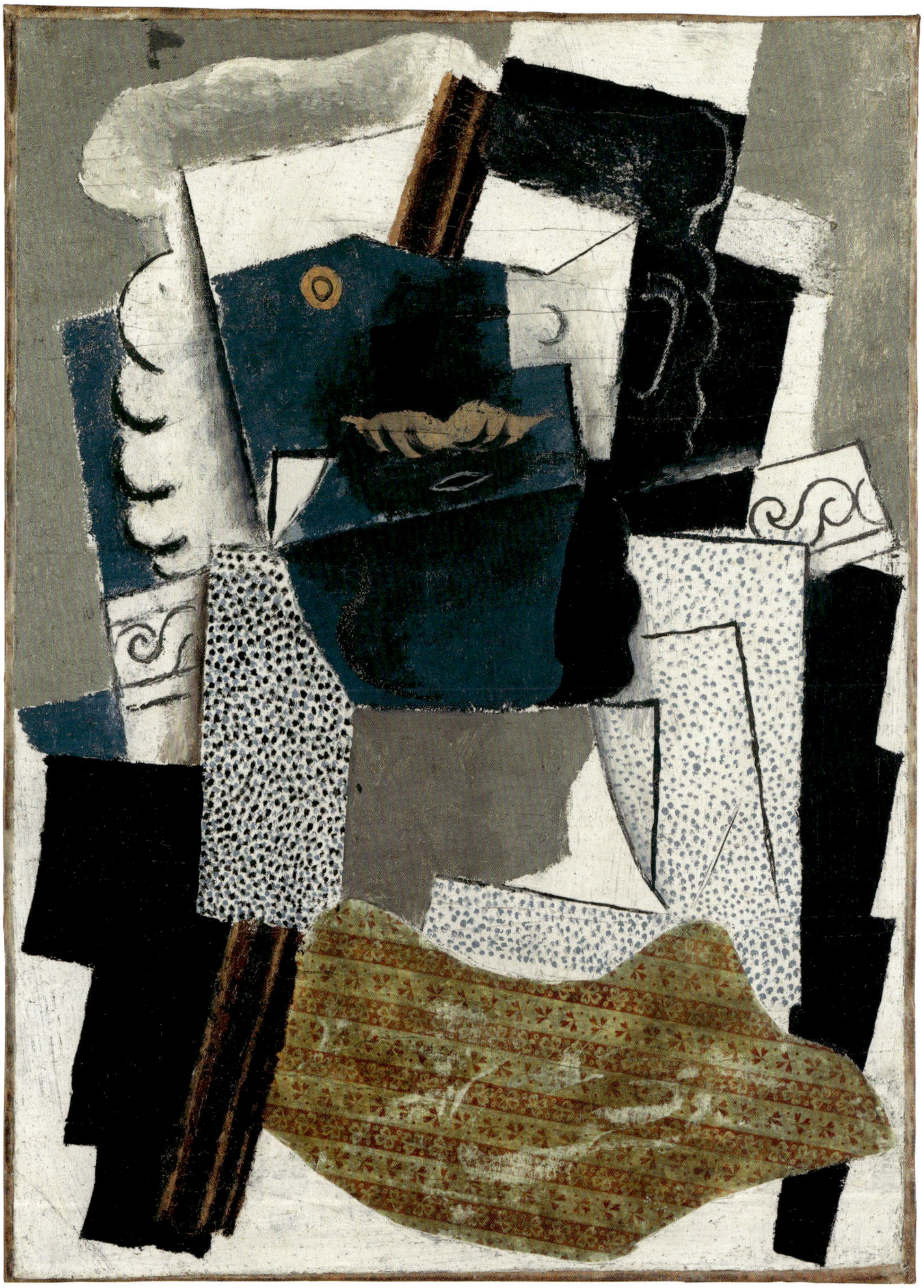

26 *Man with a Moustache*, [spring 1914]

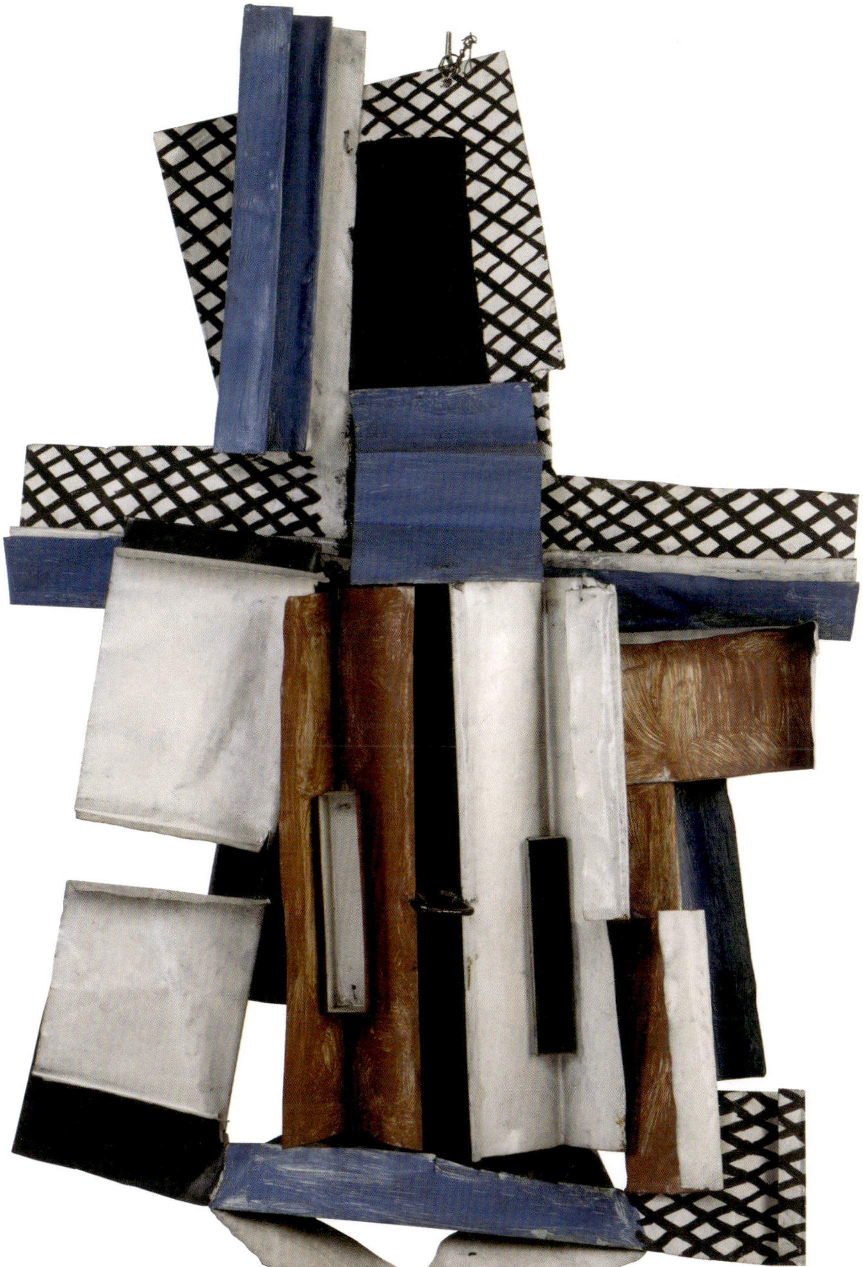

Violin, 1915

1915
1924

"When I hear people speak of the evolution of an artist, it seems to me that they are considering him standing between two mirrors that face each other and reproduce his image an infinite number of times, and that they contemplate the successive images of one mirror as his past, and the images of the other mirror as his future, while his real image is taken as his present. They do not consider that they all are the same images in different planes."

Pablo Picasso, in Marius de Zayas, "Picasso Speaks. A Statement by the Artist," *The Arts*, May 19, 1923

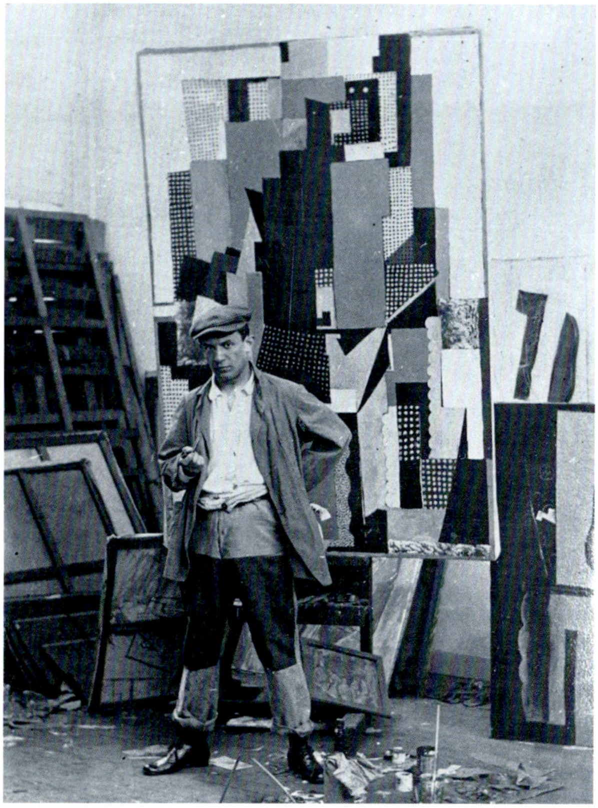

Self-portrait in front of *Man Leaning on a Table* in the studio on rue Schoelcher, 1915–16

Throughout his life, Picasso could never be pigeonholed into, nor did he ever confine himself to, a single style or movement. Even as cubism developed, he was no purist, and was prepared to employ, for his own devices, references to the modes of illusionist, naturalist representation. Integrating real objects into his works, he was also inspired by principles of modeling from photography, a technical and vernacular art form in which he had shown an interest since the beginning of the century. As for his style from 1915–24, often described as "classical," it testifies as much to Picasso's admiration of the painting of Ingres as to references to photographic studio portraiture, or the influence of Greco-Roman antiquity. By way of the pose, sinuous lines, and idealization of the model, the *Portrait d'Olga dans un fauteuil* (*Portrait of Olga in an Armchair*) harks back to the Ingresque model of *Mademoiselle Rivière* (Louvre), as well as referring to a photographic portrait of Olga taken in his studio in Montrouge. Meanwhile, *Paul en arlequin* (*Paulo as a Harlequin*) joins the procession of *infantes* painted by Velázquez, Goya, Manet, and Renoir. In both these paintings, stylistic references are skewed by the experience of the cubist collage, exacerbating the two-dimensionality of these canvases, which are, moreover, deliberately left "unfinished."

In 1921, his classical stance, which stemmed from the Pompeian experience (1917), was further nourished by the discovery of Primaticcio and Niccolò dell'Abbate, whom Picasso, staying in Fontainebleau for the summer, studied and transposed in major compositions, such as *Femmes à la fontaine* (*Women at the Fountain*) and *La Source* (*The Spring*). These paintings seem modeled out of the thick dust of charcoal and red chalk, finally coalescing like bas-reliefs in the course of obliteration.

Creating two classicizing alternatives of *Women at the Fountain* (Musée Picasso, Paris, and Museum of Modern Art, New York), Picasso simultaneously undertook two versions of *Trois musiciens* (*Three Musicians*, Museum of Modern Art, New York, and Cleveland Museum of Art), in which the cubist idiom is powerfully articulated. This duality, such as the deliberate stylistic double-dealing, remained a recurrent phenomenon in his art. It is embodied especially in the canvas, *Études* (*Studies*, [1920]). Like a banner of freedom brandished by painting, through the prism of its composition, *Studies* amalgamated cubist still life and figures, flat tints, and figures in the round, signs, and illusions, which already heralded the themes and motifs of the surrealist period.

This "classical" period in Picasso's output that focused on melancholic-looking characters of colossal form, petrified into statues, reaches its completion in the pastel on canvas, *La Danse villageoise* (*The Village Dance*, 1922), inspired by Renoir's *Danse à la campagne* (*Dance in the Country*, 1883). This period concluded in 1923, with *La Flûte de Pan* (*The Pan Flute*), a monumental canvas whose double male portrait is dedicated to the nostalgic evocation of onetime friendships with Guillaume Apollinaire and Léonide Massine. This celebration of ghosts, poets, philosophers, storytellers, and dancers heralded the reappearance of a long-faded world in blues and pinks, shot through with theatricality and teeming with mythical creatures.

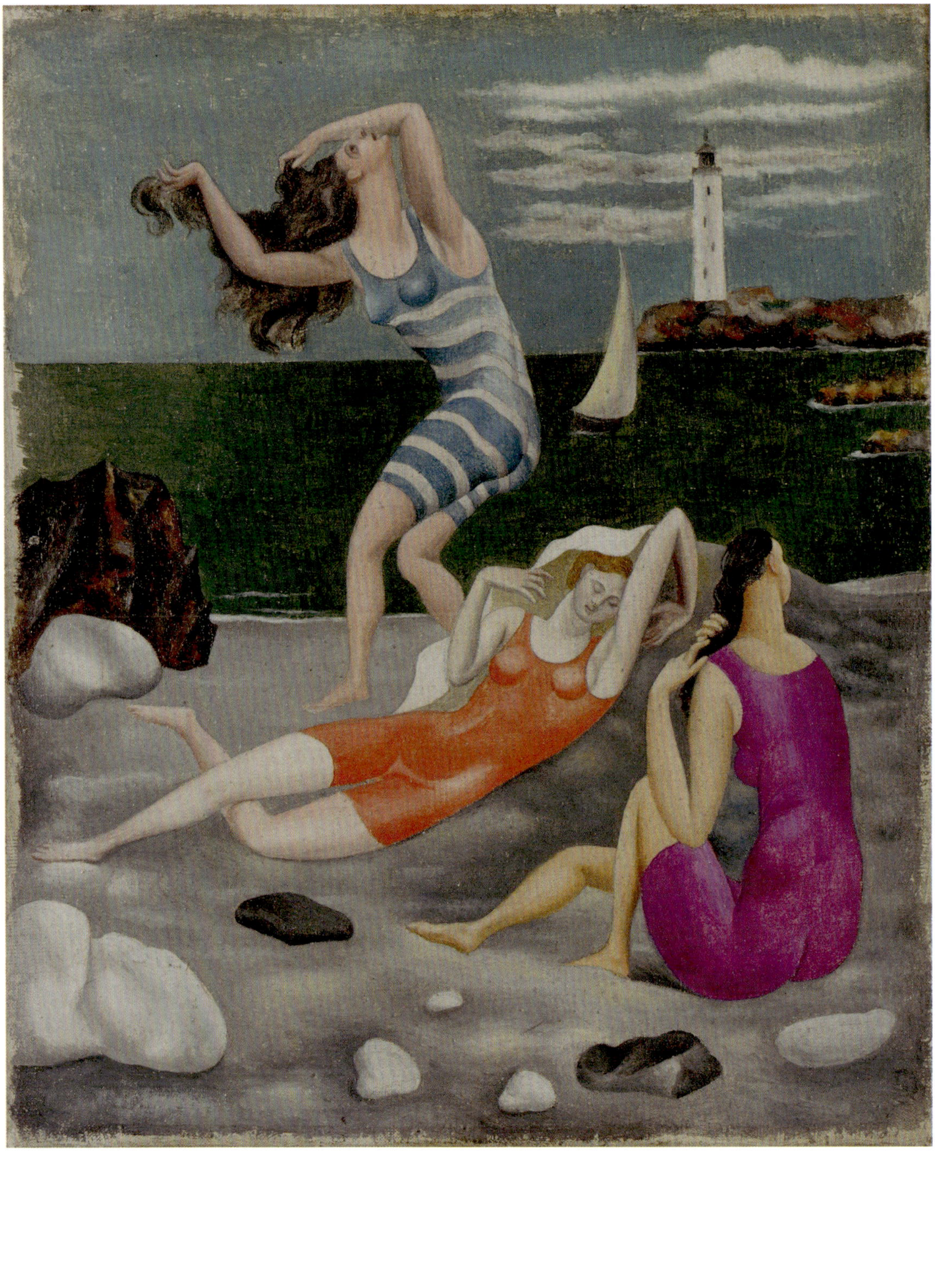

30 *Bathers*, summer 1918

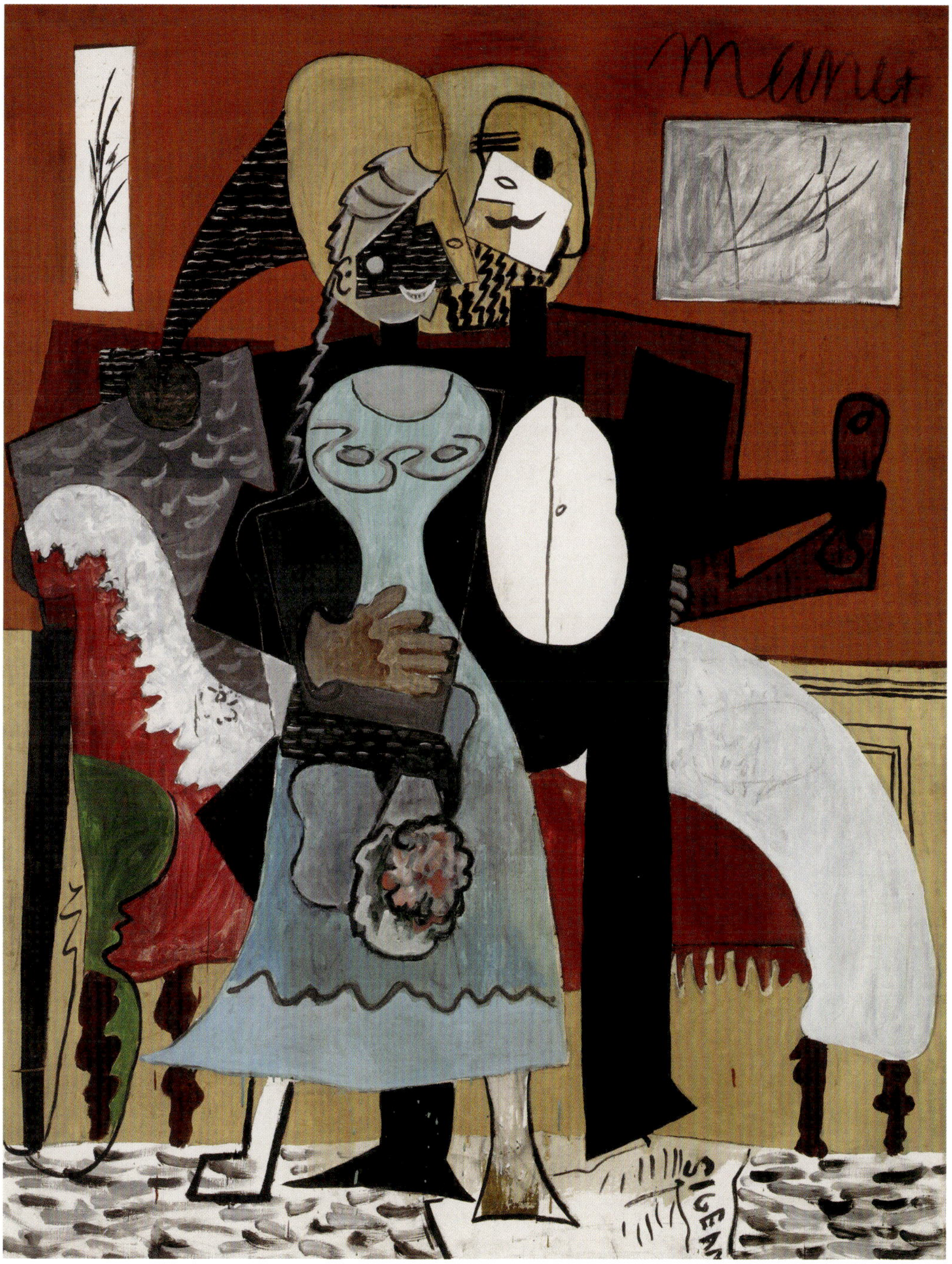

The Lovers, 1919

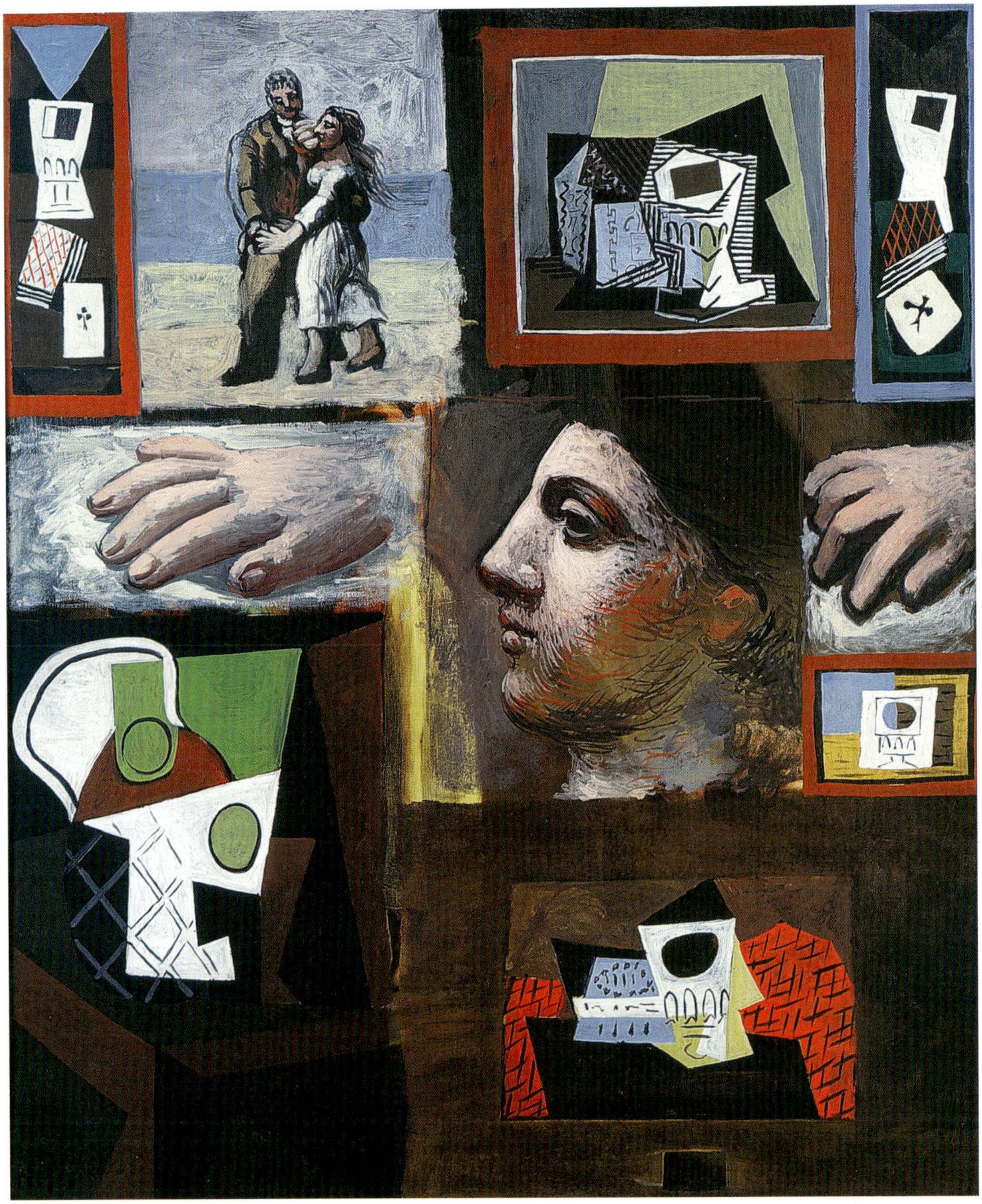

 Studies, [1920]

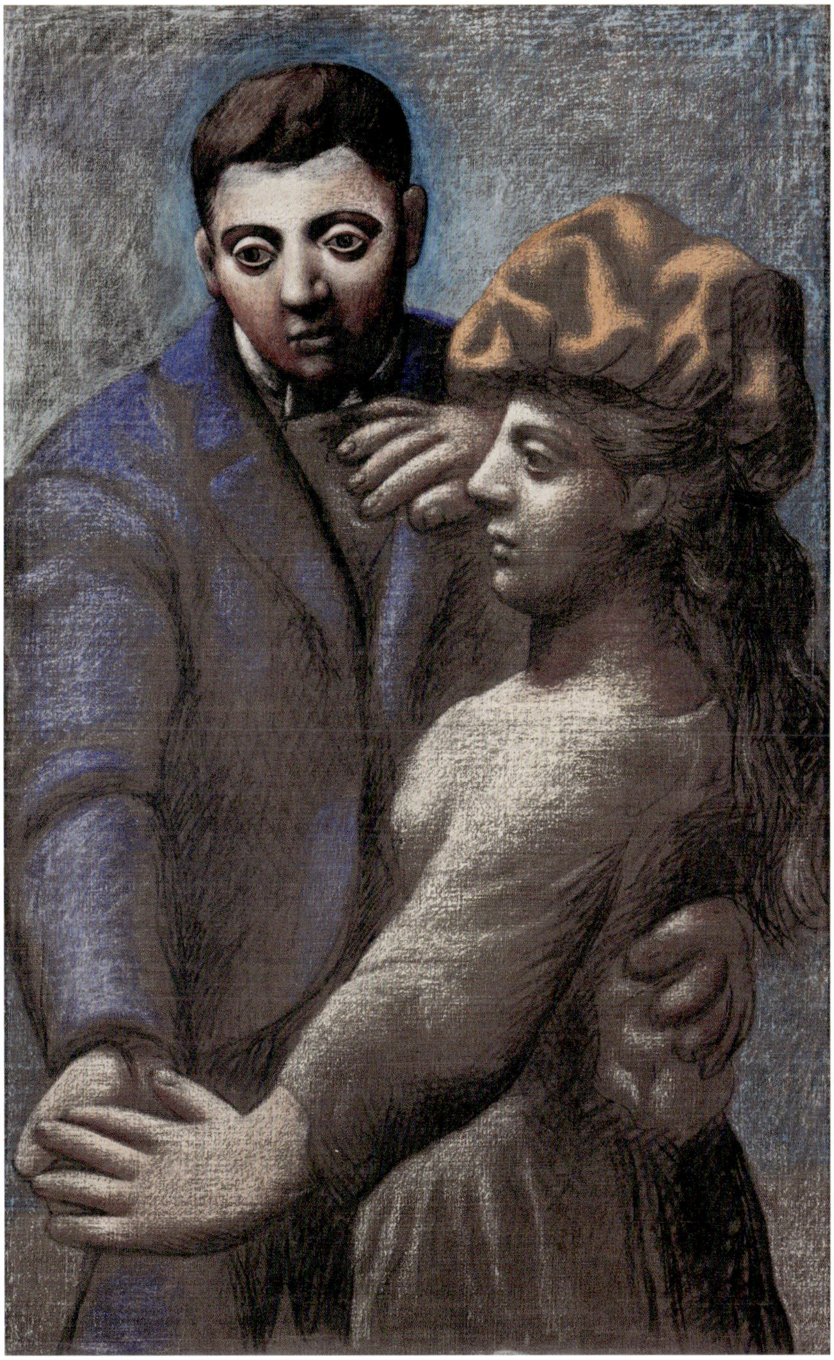

The Village Dance, 1922

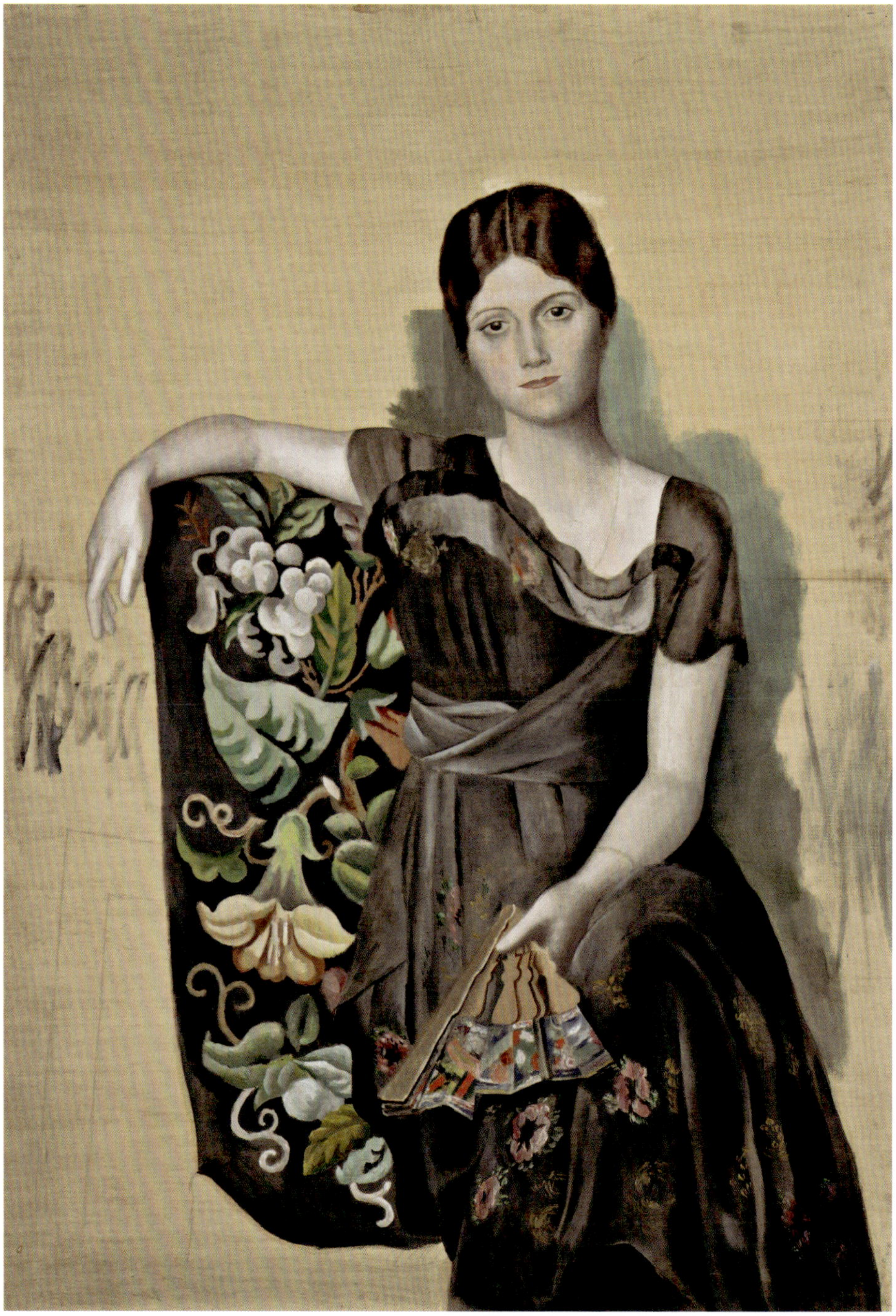

34 *Portrait of Olga in an Armchair*, spring 1918

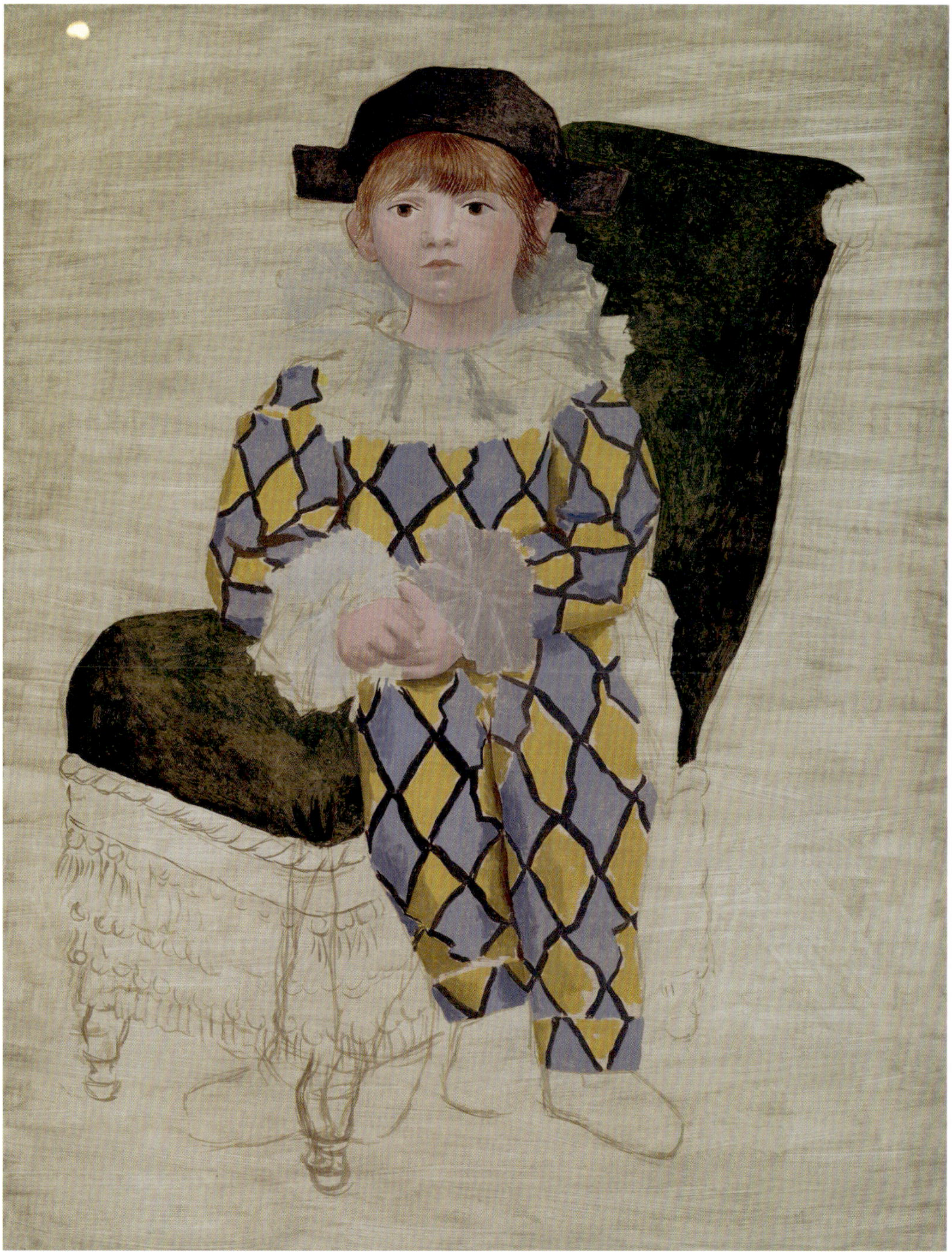

Paulo as a Harlequin, 1924

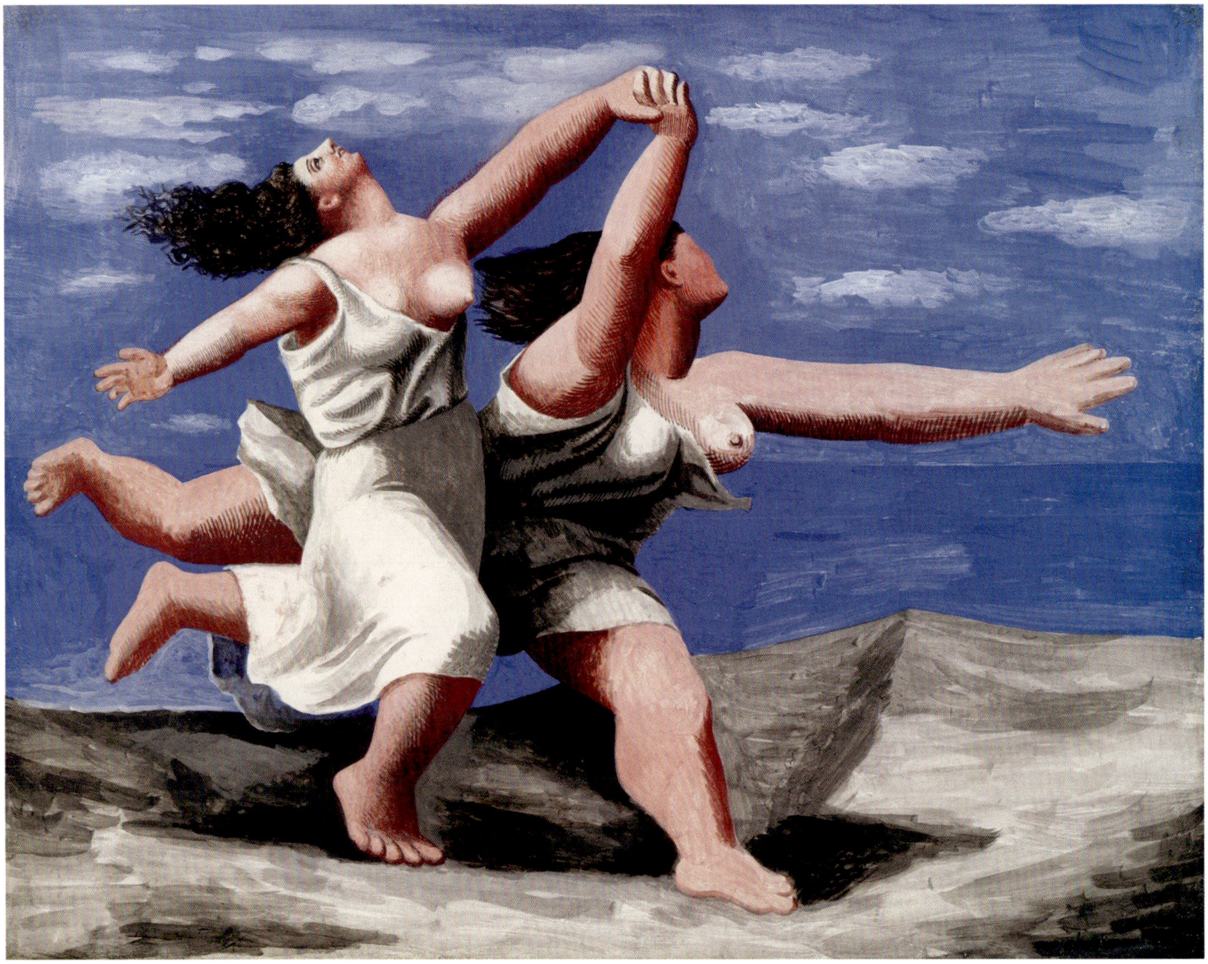

36 *Two Women Running on the Beach (The Race)*, summer 1922

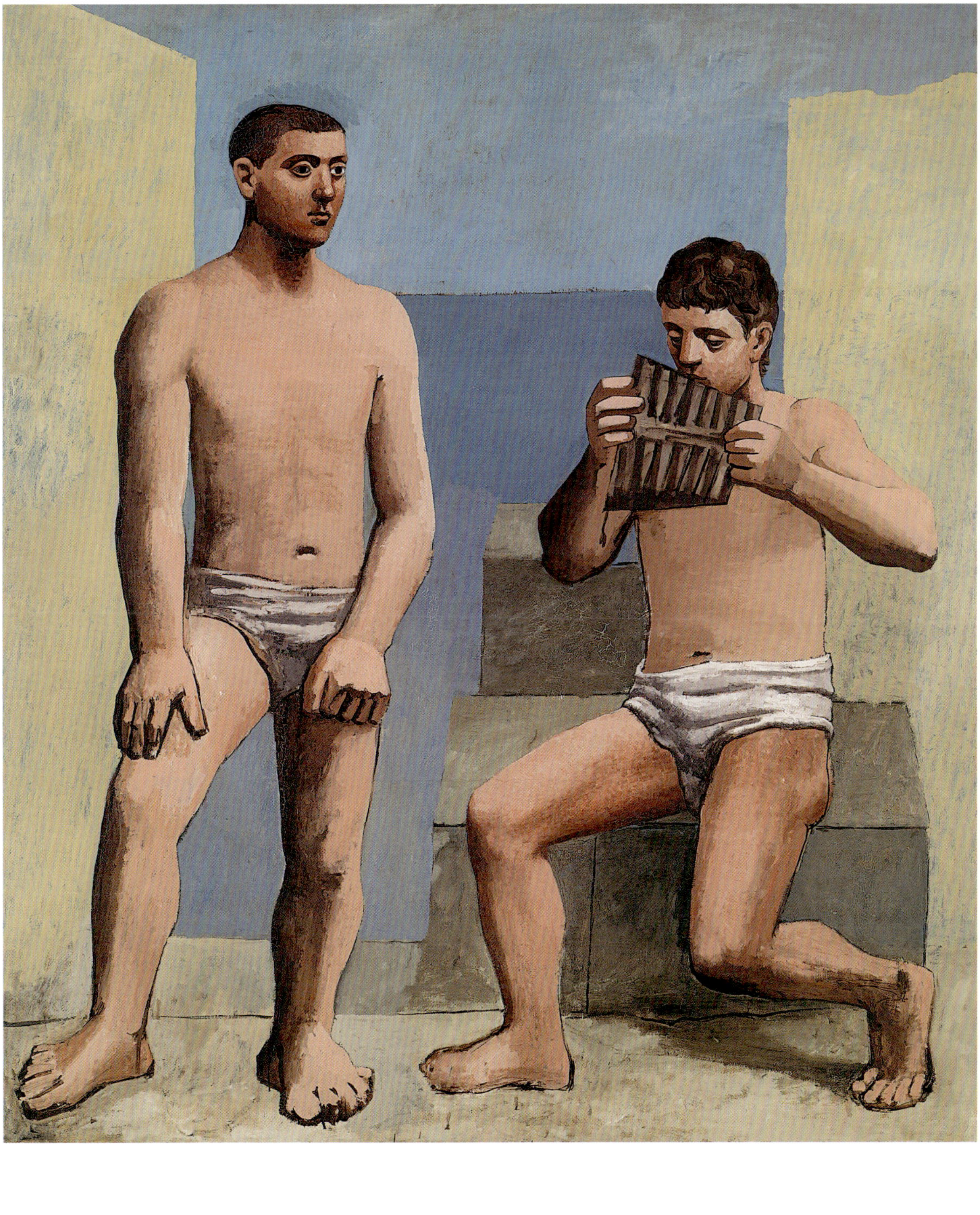

The Pan Flute, summer 1923

1924
1930

"I aim at deeper resemblance,
more real than real,
thus becoming surreal."

Pablo Picasso, in André Warnod, "En peinture, tout n'est que signe," *Arts*, June 29, 1945

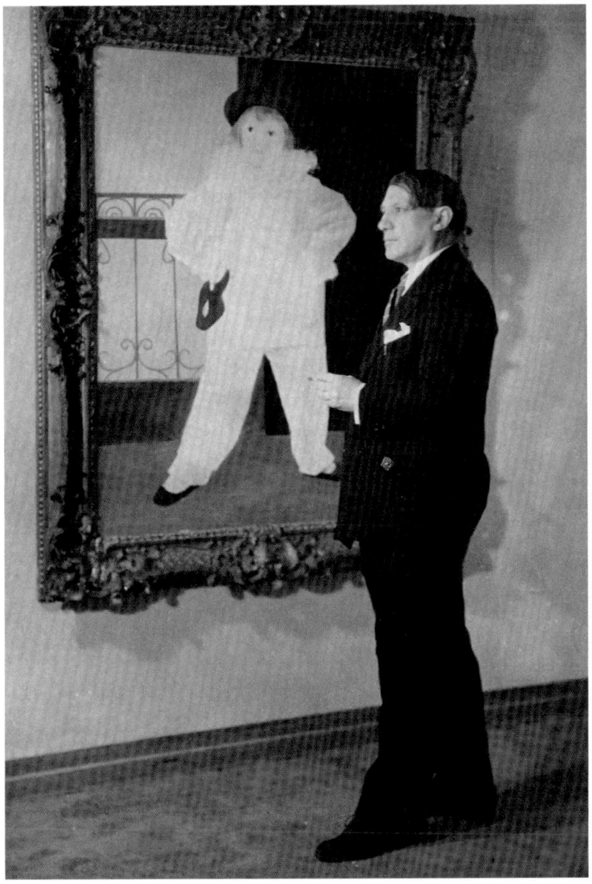

Picasso in front of *Paul as Pierrot*, Galerie Georges Petit, Paris, 1932, anonymous photographer

Picasso's surrealist phase opened with a new ballet on a mythological theme, *Mercure*, for which he created the sets, curtain, and costumes in 1924. His major compositions, such as *Mandoline sur une table* (*Mandolin on a Table*, 1924), and *Le Peintre et son modèle* (*The Painter and His Model*, 1926), bent the cubist grid into a new, curvilinear idiom. It imposed a new dynamic of contortion, typical of the calligraphic transformation his oeuvre was on the brink of making. Transposing onto canvas the principle of automatic writing preached by surrealism, Picasso embarked on a search for images from the unconscious. The kisses, the little bathers playing ball, the polymorphic acrobats, the women swimming—all signaled the emergence of these oneiric creatures in the artist's output.

The series of *Studios*, with *Nu sur fond blanc* (*Nude on White Background*, 1927) and *Peintre à la palette et au chevalet* (*Painter with Palette and Easel*, 1928), which are contemporary with the sequence of etchings, *La Suite Vollard* (The Vollard Suite), enacts the optical triangulation of the relations established between the painter/sculptor, his model, and the work in progress. As in a kind of pictorial theorem, this confrontation opposed naturalist reality and cubist interpretation, as well as sculpture and painting. Hovering on the threshold of the picture, the painter represents himself as a mediator in *Figure et profil* (*Figure and Profile*, 1928), where he maintains the delicate balance between two antagonistic worlds.

In 1928, Picasso modeled anthropomorphic sculptures titled *Métamorphose I* and *II* (*Metamorphosis I* and *II*) that constituted his earliest studies for *Le Monument à Apollinaire* (*Monument to Apollinaire*), a project that had been awarded to him by the Comité Apollinaire in 1921. Picasso, with the assistance of his friend, sculptor Julio González, was to realize many wire models like "drawings in space." The technique of cutout and welded metal had produced significant sculptures in the past in Picasso's oeuvre, such as *Violon* (*Violin*, 1915), and *Guitare* (*Guitar*, 1924). *La Femme au jardin* (*The Woman in the Garden*, 1929) and *Tête de femme* (*Head of a Woman*, 1929–30), incorporated household items or metal brackets, conferring a novel, poetical, monumental aspect to the project.

The artist pursued the equivalences between the fields of sculpture and painting when in 1929 he applied the same logic of production to *La Femme au jardin* (*The Woman in the Garden*) and *Grand nu au fauteuil rouge* (*Large Nude in a Red Armchair*), which share a similar program for enacting weightlessness: a sculpture spun out of emptiness, composed of bars and scrap metal painted white, projecting a spectral shadow on the wall; this disturbing entity, languid, erectile, brazenly exposes its naked anatomy in a decor saturated with signs. Heads with sewn-up mouths, with scars of sand, looking out of the corner of their eye, take up where these metaphorical creatures left off to exemplify those metamorphoses to which Picasso's oeuvre would from then on be devoted.

The temptation of abstraction that haunted his work since the beginning of cubism is here reaffirmed with unprecedented power. Picasso's determination to account for the signs inherent in things and beings led him to synthesize—in both his sculpture and painting—cryptograms, paraphs, and chrisms, through which the most vehement language infiltrated the image.

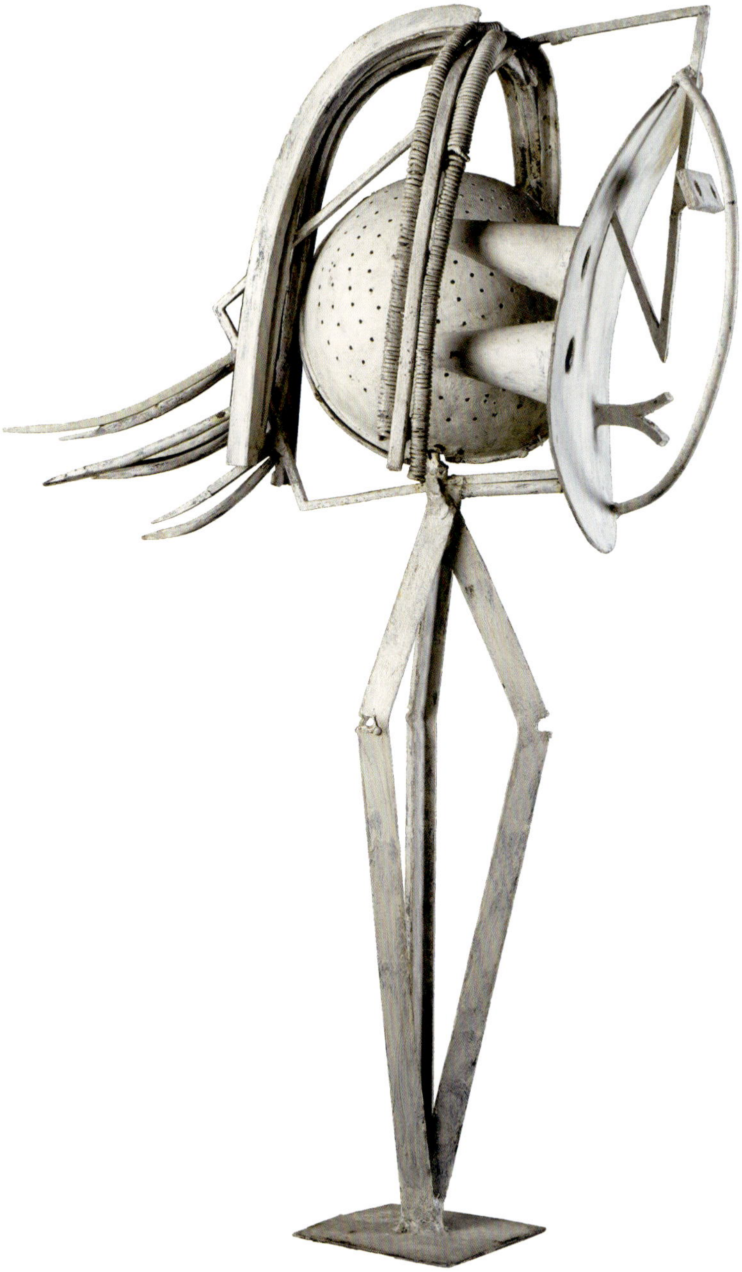

40 *Head of a Woman*, 1929–30

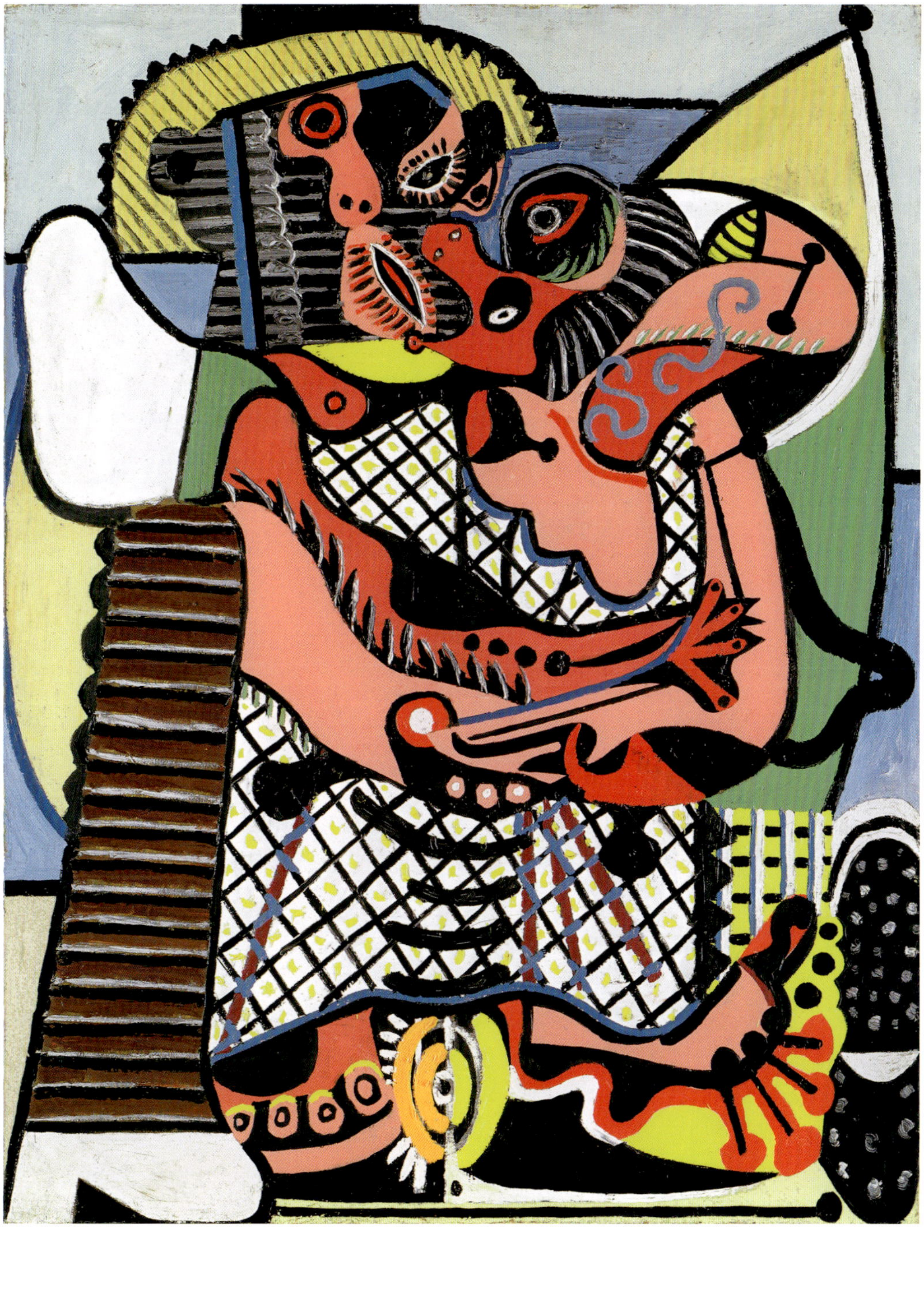

The Kiss, summer 1925

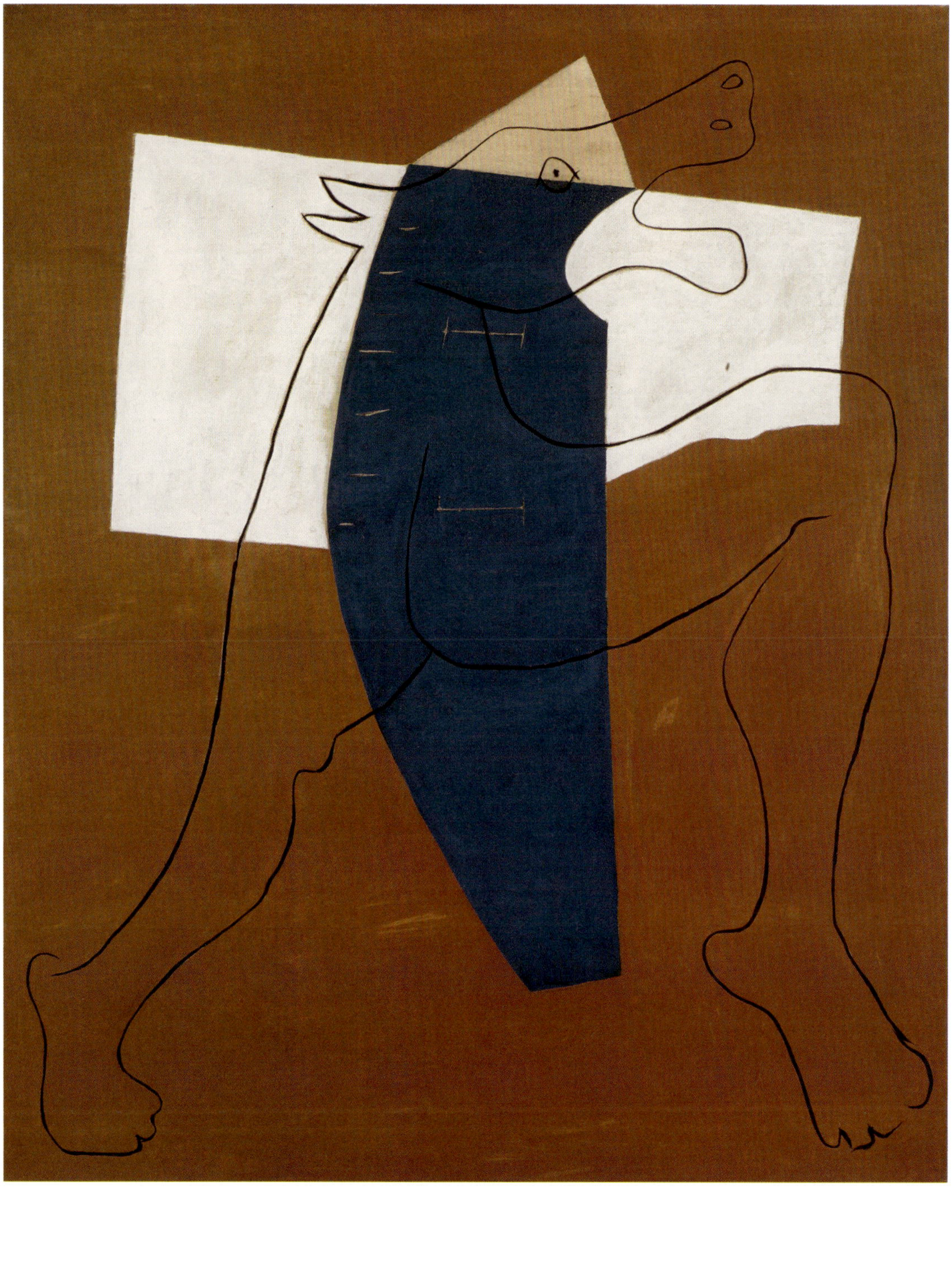

42 *Running Minotaur*, April 1928

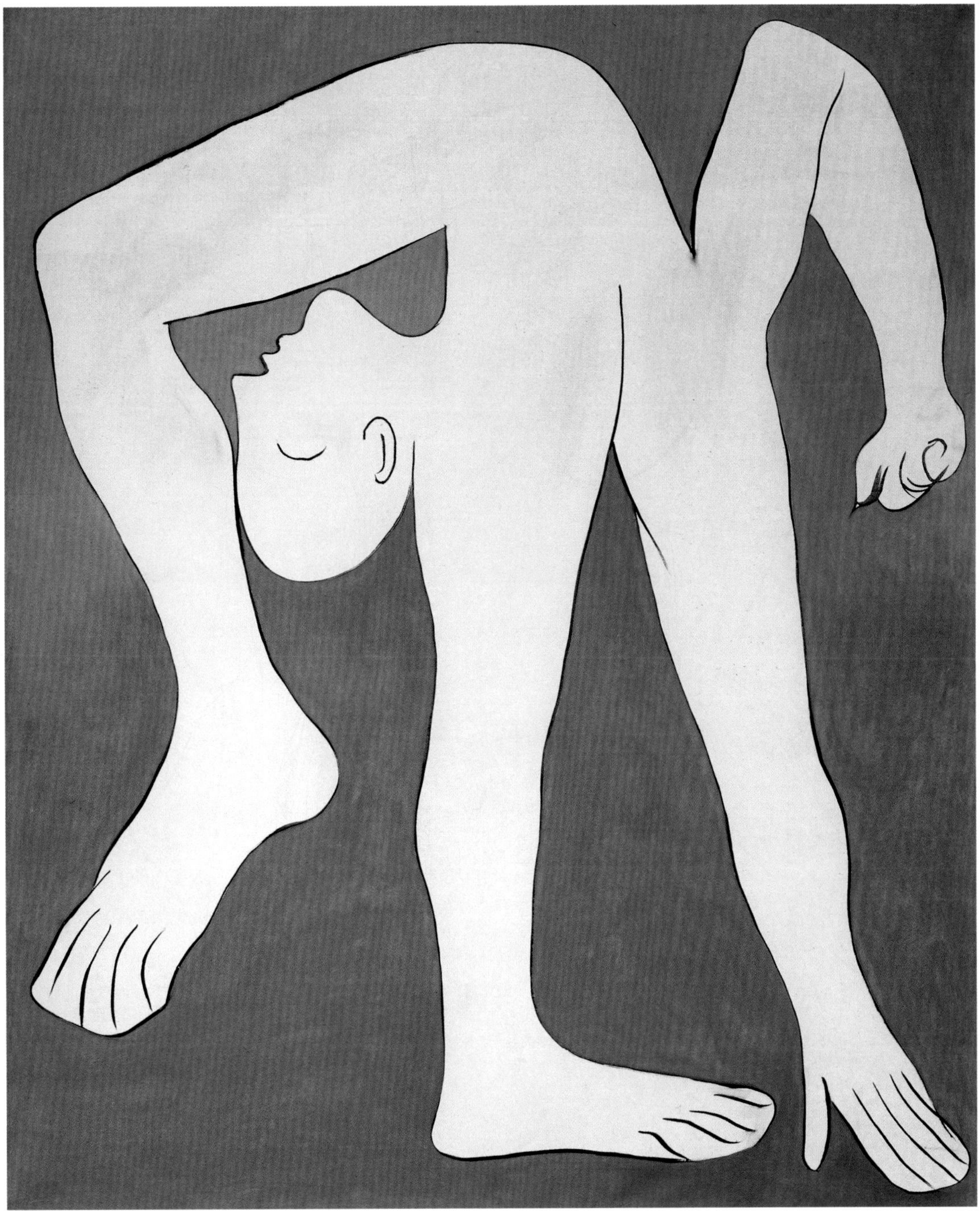

The Acrobat, January 18, 1930

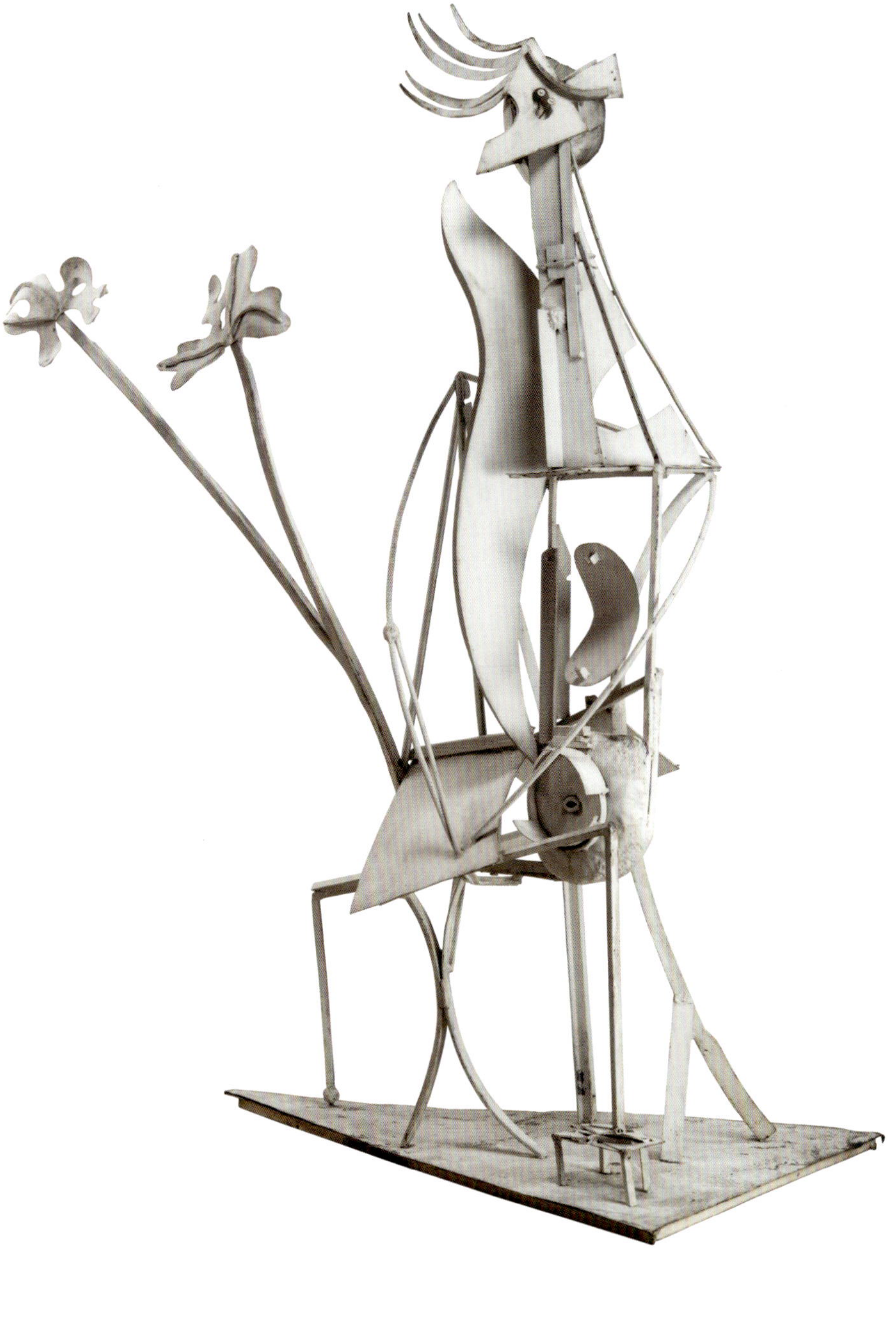

44 *The Woman in the Garden*, spring 1929

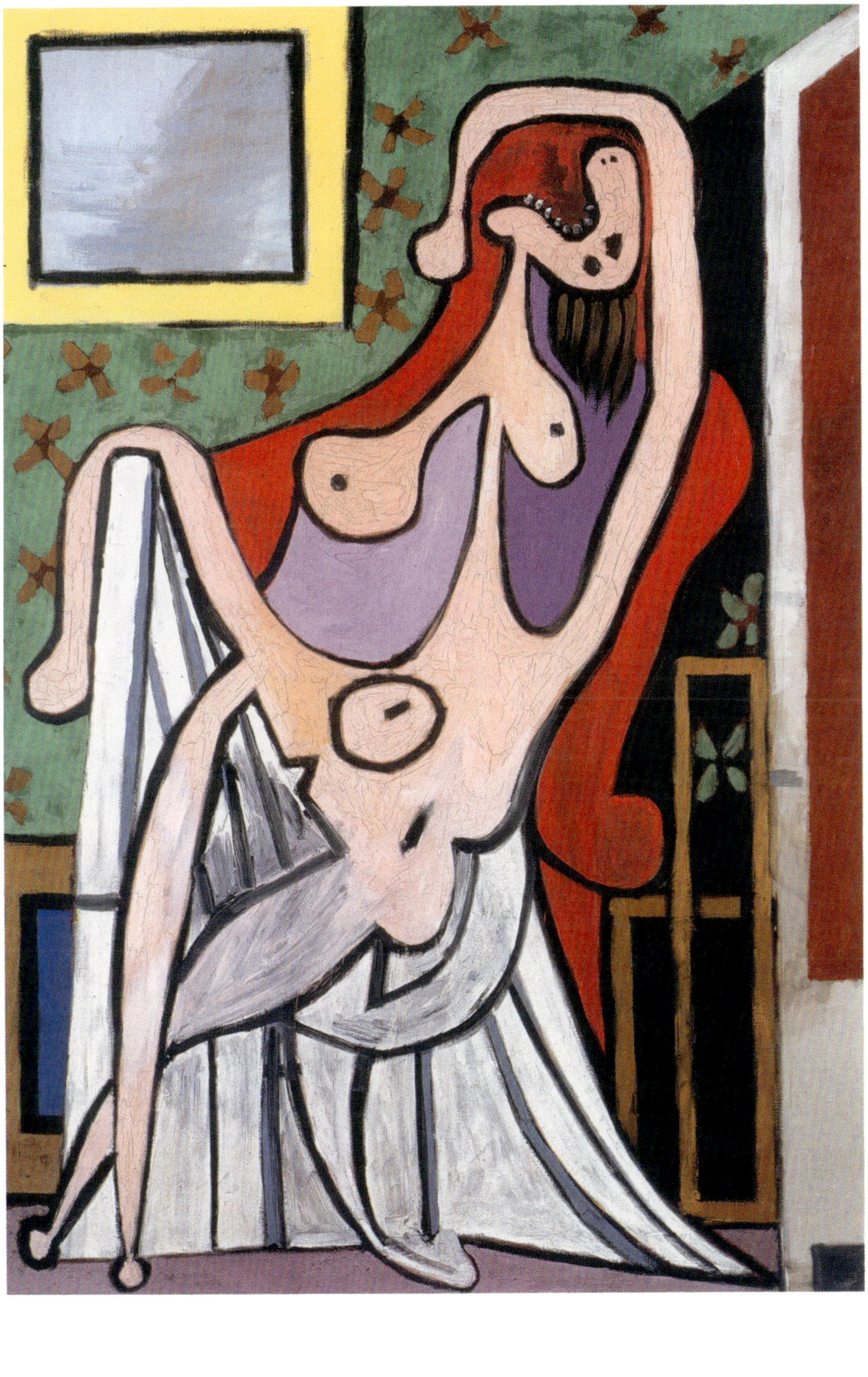

Large Nude in a Red Armchair, May 5, 1929

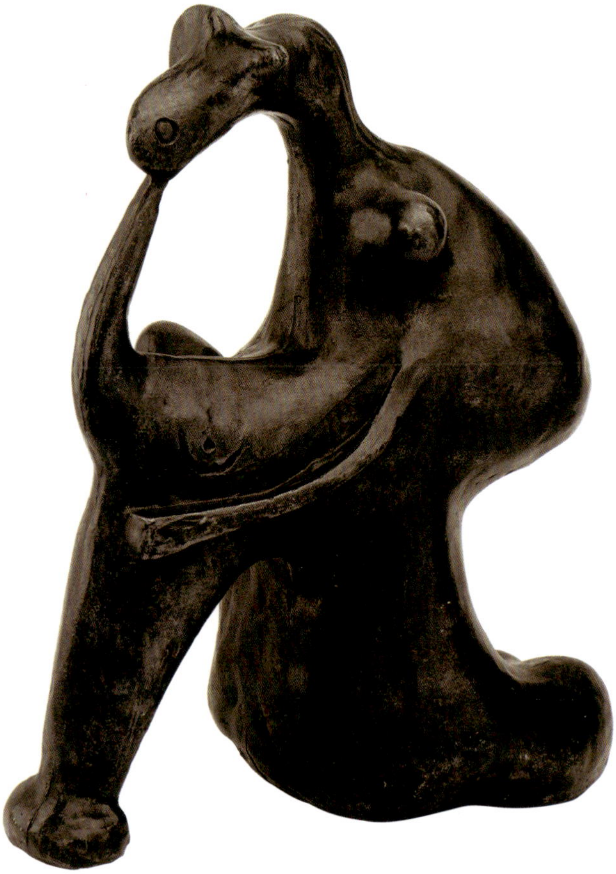

46 *Metamorphosis II*, 1928

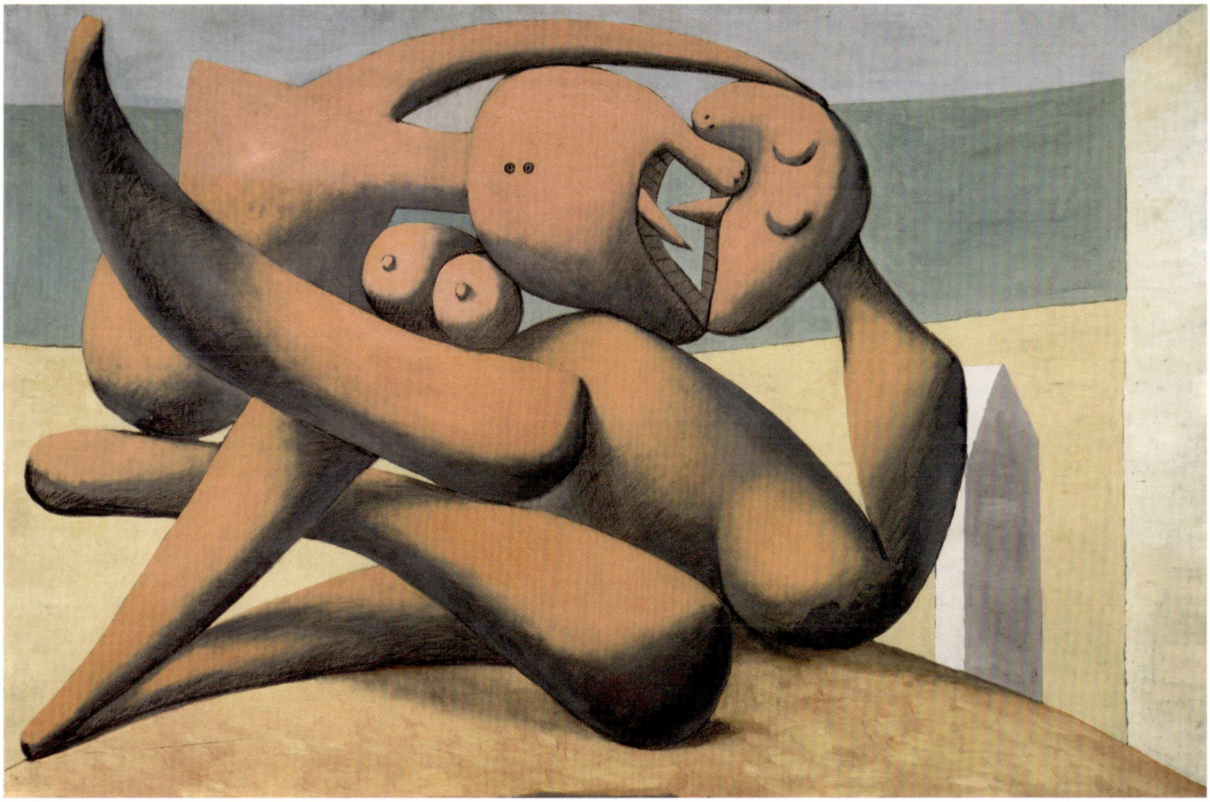

Figures on the Seashore, January 12, 1931

1930
1936

"If all the roads I have been down were marked on a map and joined up with a line, would it not represent a Minotaur?"

Pablo Picasso, in Romuald Dor de la Souchère, "Picasso in Antibes," *The Burlington Magazine,* originally published in French as *Picasso à Antibes*, (Paris: Hazan, 1960)

By the beginning of the 1920s, the mythographic references had become central to Picasso's oeuvre. Myth imposed itself as the preeminent operational dimension to establish, articulate, and consolidate the entire process of artistic creation. The chief purpose of such narratives was to establish a history of the creation of the cosmos, with its gods, its humans, and its animals. Ovid's *Metamorphoses*, which Picasso illustrated in 1931, is a poetical compilation of legends dating back to the archaic period of Greece. These legends of immortalization and gender change take humanity as a starting point for metamorphoses destined to people the world: "transformations"—into birds, winged insects, animals, plants, rocks or stones, stars, and echoes.

Inverting its meaning, Picasso embraced the opening sentence with which Ovid presents the "argument" of his cycle of poems: "I wish to speak of metamorphoses of forms into new bodies, since the most remote origins of the world until my own time." Conversely, the painter's aim was to pursue—in hitherto unexplored ways—the transmutation of "bodies" into "new forms." Picasso confers on myth a capacity to express "the indecent, the incongruous, the sacrilegious." He described his project to André Malraux: "To displace. To put eyes into legs. To contradict.... Nature does many things I do. She hides them! She must be made to show them." (*Picasso's Mask*, 1976). Thus, during the 1930s, Picasso's work became a locus for the epiphany of the unknown, the forbidden; on the border between automatic image, somnambulism, and technical chance.

In modeling the sculptural features of his favorite model of the time, the young Marie-Thérèse Walter, whom he met in 1927, the artist reverted to plaster. Accentuating her salient features, he combined curves and volumes in the series of large *Heads* at Boisgeloup. These sculptures exemplify the work of schematization and abstraction of the human form. Such aims are particularly relevant to the abstract version of *Tête de femme* (*Head of a Woman*, 1931), a veritable mechanism of volume suspended in space, as well as in the semantic accumulation of *Buste de femme* (*Bust of a Woman*, 1931), evocative of some neolithic totem. In sculpture, painting, and printmaking, during the surrealist period Picasso once again deployed a multivalent language, with academic figuration in the antique style, the sign patterns of cubism, and the physical deformation of surrealism. The combination of found objects, interred in ductile material, such as sand, earth, or plaster, or else enmeshed in cocoons of wire, generates—as in *Composition au gant* (*Composition with Glove*, 1930) and *Figure* (1935)—novel, fantastic images. Thus, after appealing to the object to introduce reality itself into the cubist work, in the dreamlike compositions of 1930–35 its material presence injected the "uncanny" nature of "sur-reality" into the core of the creative process.

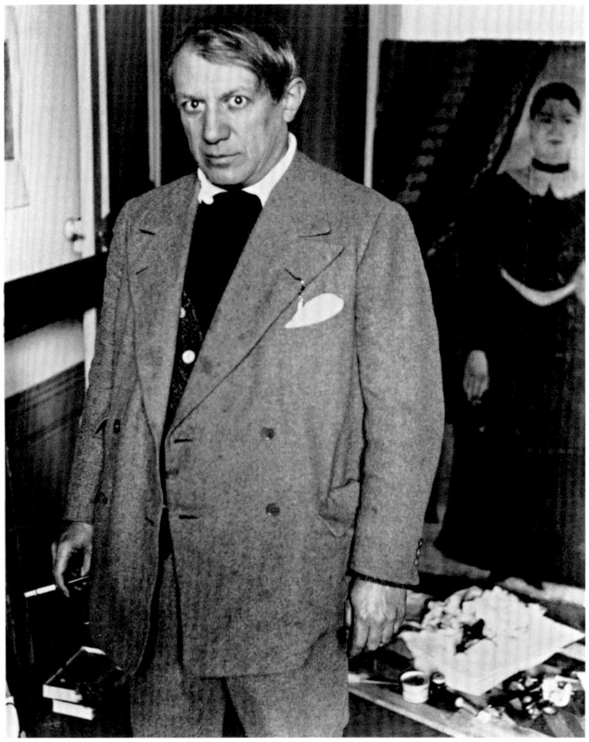

Picasso in front of *Portrait de femme*
by the Douanier Rousseau, 1932, by Brassaï

The generative icon of this period, the Minotaur, appeared for the first time in a large collage and a painting from 1928 entitled *Minotaure* (*Minotaur*, Musée National d'Art Moderne and Musée Picasso, Paris). During the years 1928–38, this mythological figure, son of Pasiphae and Jupiter, abandoned in the depths of Minos' labyrinth, came to occupy a central role in Picasso's oeuvre. Revealed as the artist's alter ego, Picasso puts on a mask so as to play out his obsessions and fears. Grafting an animal head onto a man's body, for the surrealists the Minotaur is the incarnation of the ambiguous state of humanity, subjected to unconscious impulses, to the pleasure principle, to the death instinct. For Picasso, it symbolized the tension between instinct and reason that was discharged in a rich sequence of works, ranging from corridas and dead bullfighters of both sexes, painted, engraved, or drawn between 1933–36, to the painting *Minotaure au javelot* (*Minotaur with Javelin*, 1934), the large-scale bronze, *Tête de taureau* (*Head of a Bull*, 1931), and the sequence of prints and gouaches of *La Minotauromachie* (*The Minotauromachy*), 1935–36, with which the mythographic cycle concluded. From the outbreak of the Spanish Civil War in 1936 to the dark years that saw the rise of fascism in Europe, the inner combat intensified, conferring a contemporary dramatization on the archaism of the theme.

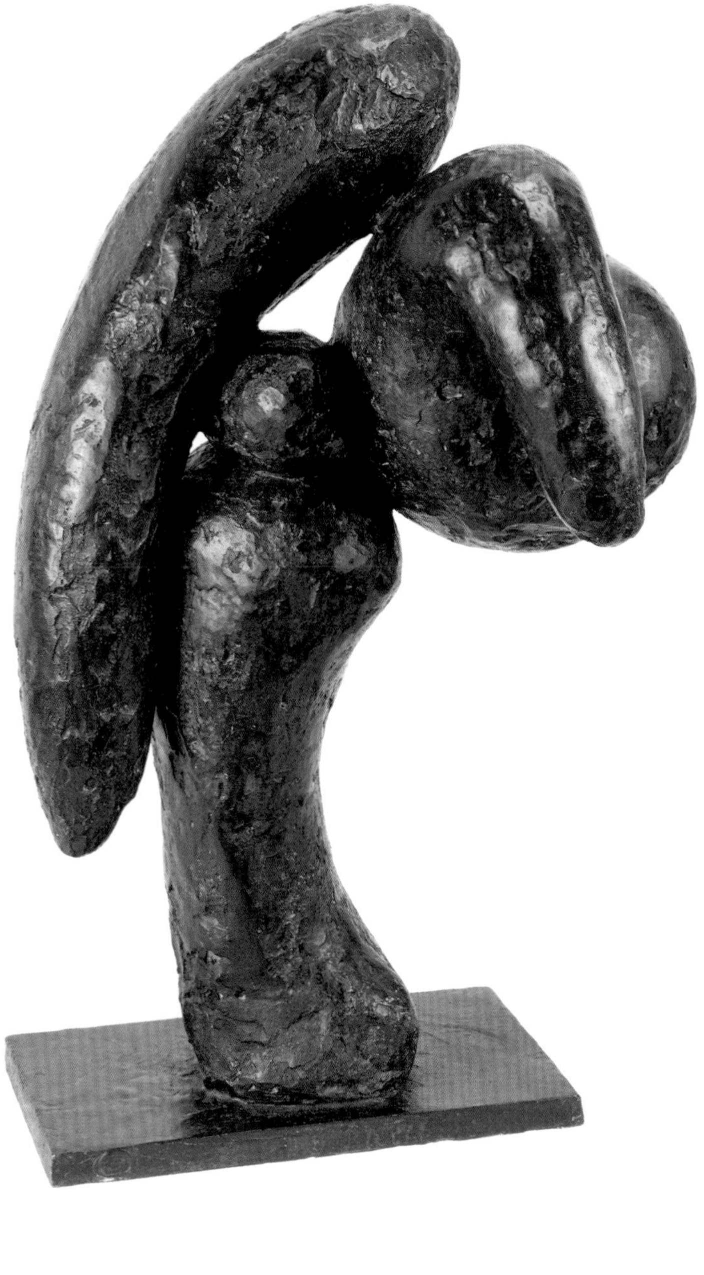

50 *Head of a Woman*, 1931

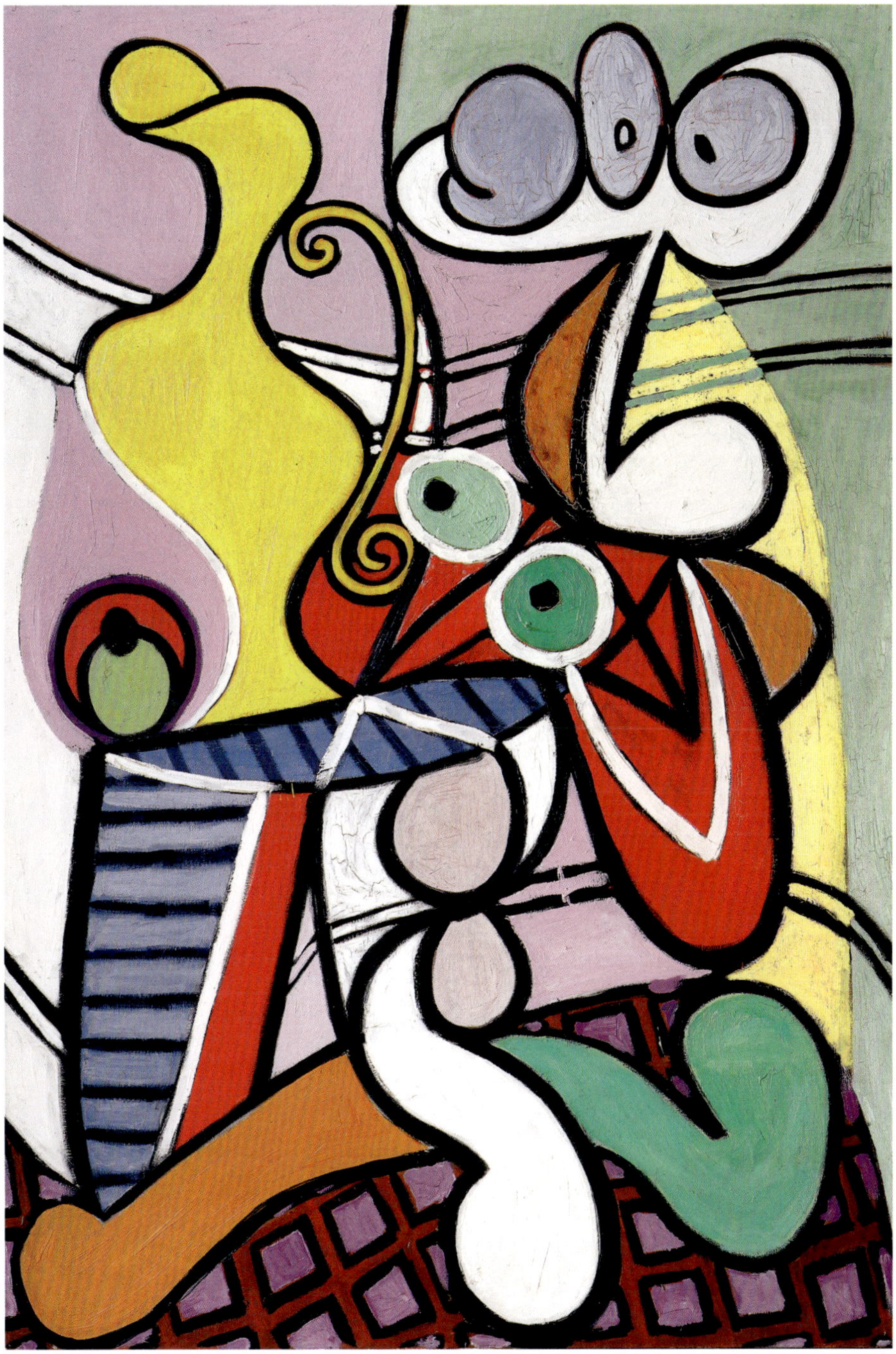

Large Still Life with a Pedestal Table, March 11, 1931

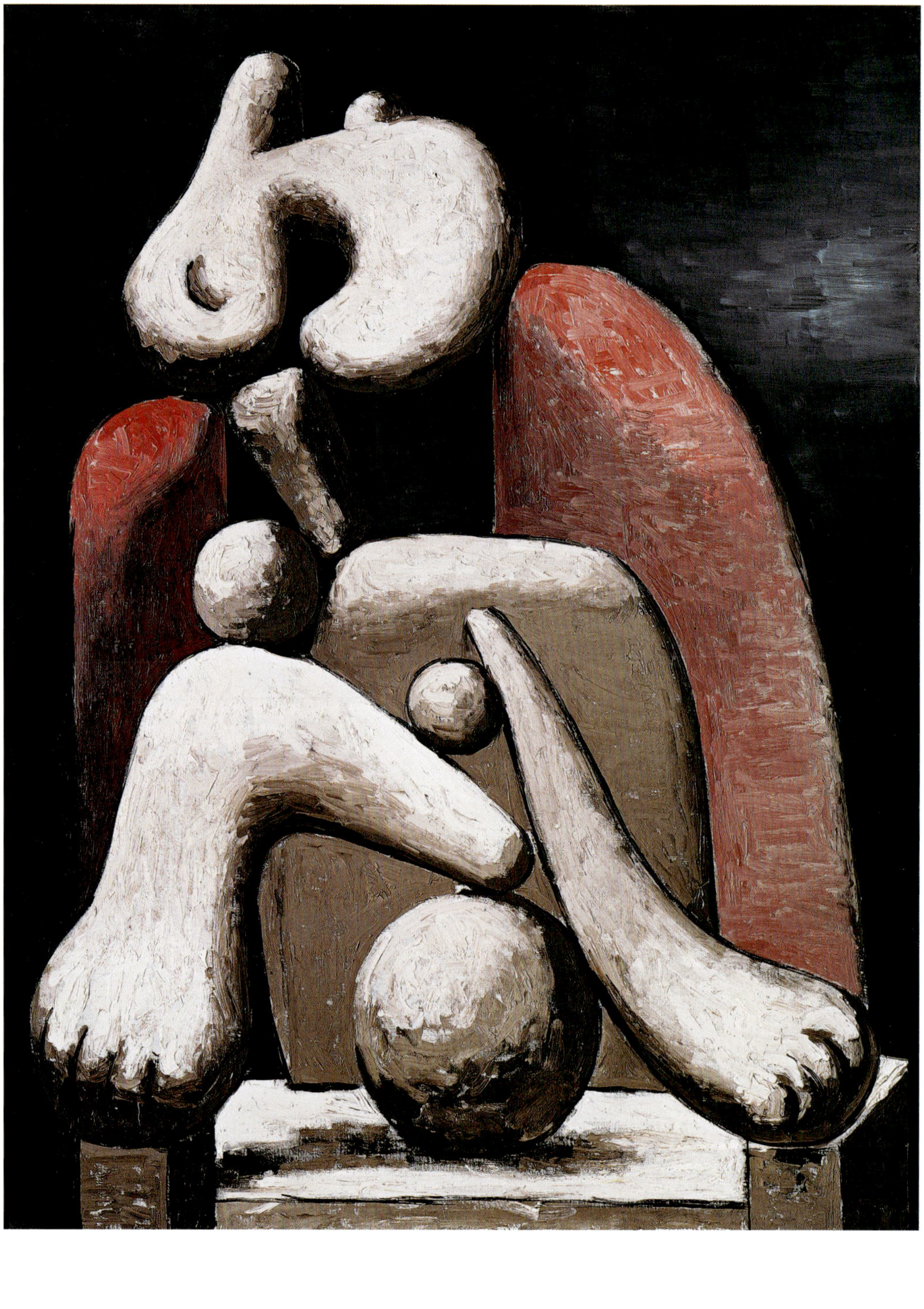

52 *Woman in a Red Armchair*, January 27, 1932

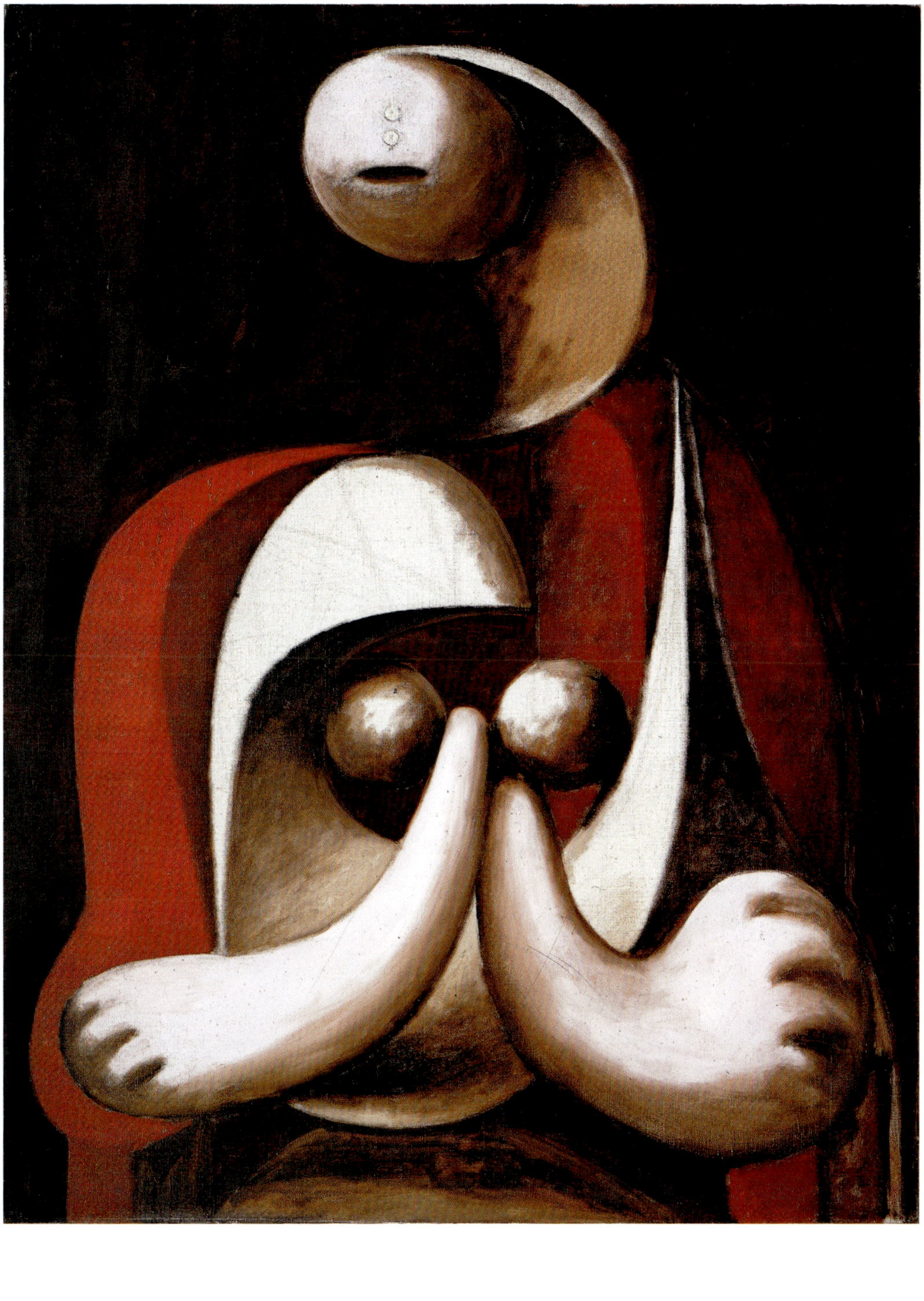

Woman Sitting in a Red Armchair, 1932

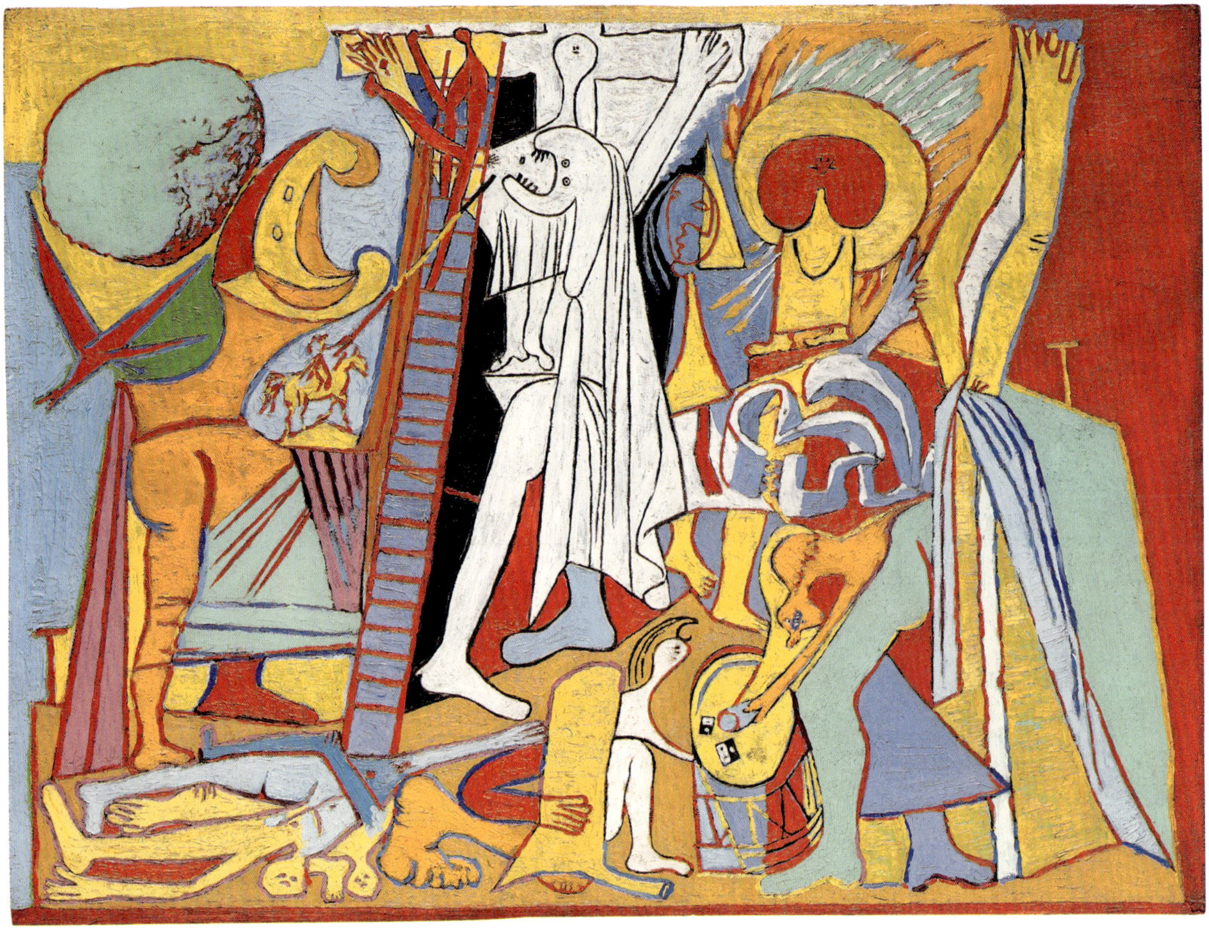

 Crucifixion, February 7, 1930

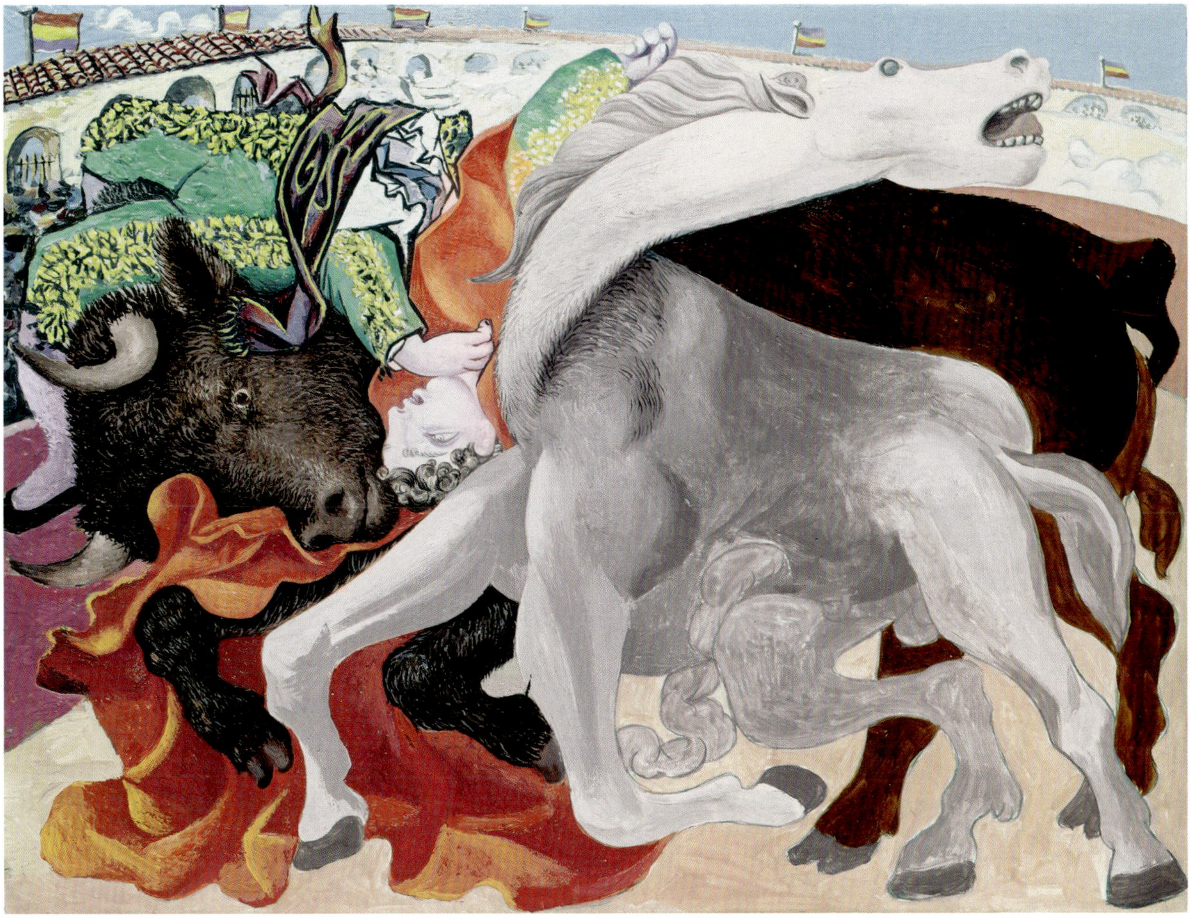

Bullfight: The Death of the Torero, September 19, 1933

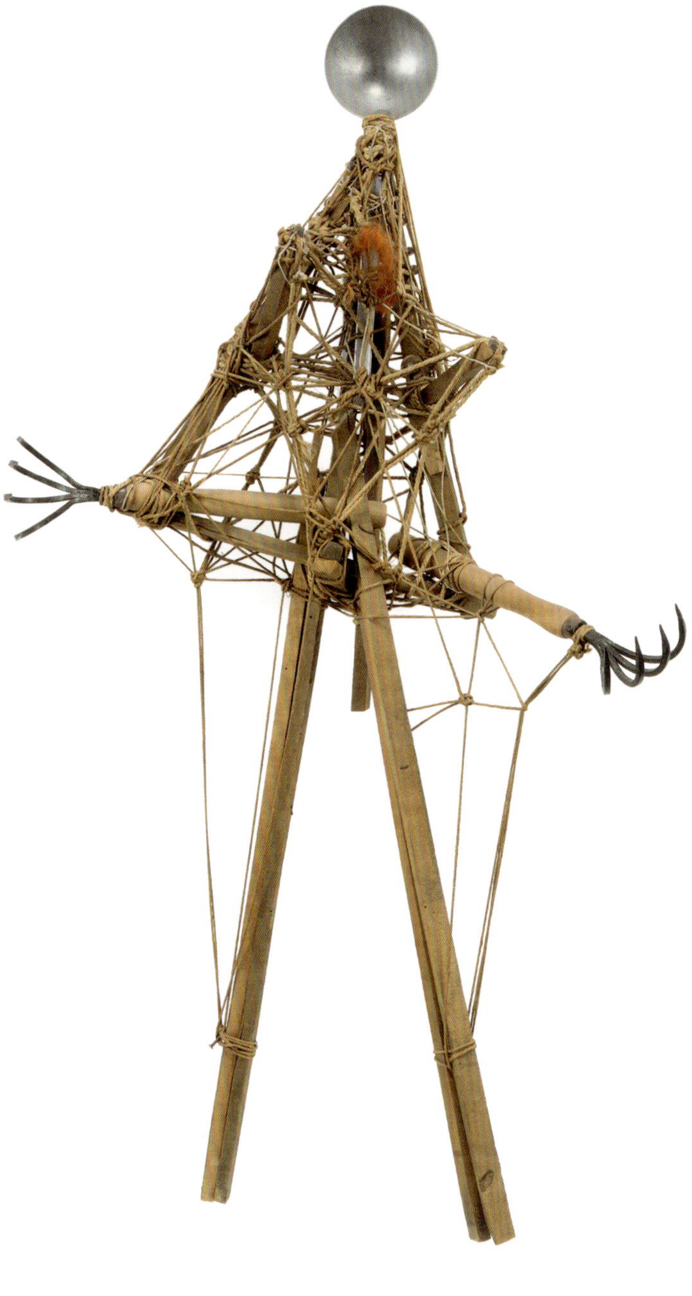

56 *Figure*, 1935

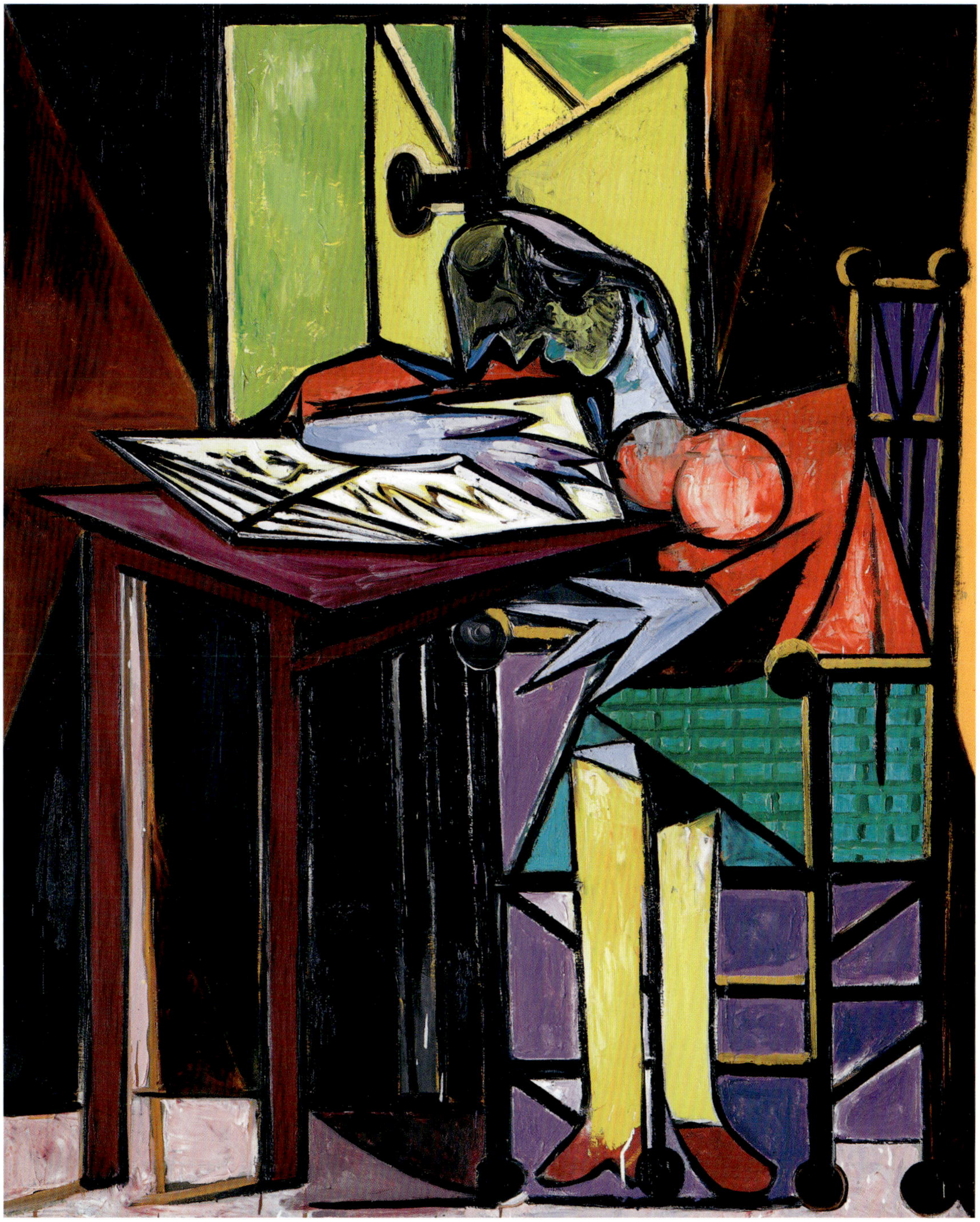

Woman Reading, January 9, 1935

1936
1939

"Cries of children cries of women cries of birds cries of flowers cries of wood and stone cries of brick cries of furniture of beds of chairs of curtains of casseroles of cats and paper cries of smells that claw themselves of smoke that gnaws the neck of cries that boil in cauldron and the rain of birds that floods the sea that eats into the bone and breaks the teeth biting the cotton that the sun wipes on its plate that bourse and bank hide in the footprint left embedded in the rock."

Pablo Picasso, poem in Spanish, June 15–18, 1937, in *Picasso, Écrits*, (Paris: RMN, Gallimard, 1989)

Picasso was a committed Republican; the Spanish Civil War inspired works that he conceived as expressly "propagandist." Simultaneously, the artist threw himself into projects promoting art and culture, launched by the Popular Front government in France. He wanted to "commit" to the contemporary political struggle in contributing to history as it unfolded. His curtain for Romain Rolland's play *Le 14 Juillet* (*The Fourteenth of July*), which returned to and further developed the motif of a gouache, *La Dépouille du Minotaure en costume d'arlequin* (*The Corpse of the Minotaur in Harlequin Costume*), falls under his will for an art of commitment.

Appointed honorary director of the Prado Museum in 1936, Picasso engraved a series of vignettes, *Songe et mensonge de Franco* (*Dream and Lie of Franco*), with the intention of printing them in a postcard format to fund the Republican struggle. Called upon to create a large-scale piece for the Spanish Pavilion at the 1937 Exposition Internationale des Arts et des Techniques in Paris, the original concept was for a panel on the theme of the painter and his model—as demonstrated by a number of studies in the Musée Picasso. Shortly after the bombardment of the Basque city of Guernica, on April 26, 1937, by the Nazi air force in support of the pro-Franco opposition, the picture underwent a total transformation. Later titled *Guernica* (Centro de Arte Reina Sofia, Madrid), Picasso's canvas, a large grisaille, as if built up of layers of signs lifted from press pictures and typography, would become the manifesto of twentieth-century *engagé* painting. Unveiled in Paris, and surrounded by about sixty painted and drawn preparatory studies, in 1937–38 it became the object of a traveling exhibit aimed at mobilizing the population in the defense of the Spanish Republic.

La femme qui pleure (*The Weeping Woman*, 1937), is also part of this sequence full of pathos in which Picasso borrows themes of lamentation from devotional painting. He declared: "For me, Dora is a woman who weeps. This was Dora's deepest reality." (Françoise Gilot and Carlton Lake, *Life with Picasso*, 1964). The pictorial motif of lamentation is echoed in the figure of the *Homme suppliant* (*Suppliant Man*), which adopts an exaggerated pose derived from Spanish Gothic and baroque, and possesses the characteristic features of the painter. A profound empathy grips Picasso when he reuses the figure of *La femme qui pleure* or the emblematic *Suppliante* (*The Suppliant*) throughout 1937, a painting based on photographs by the Catalan photographer Agustí Centelles, taken during the bombing of Lerida in early November 1937.

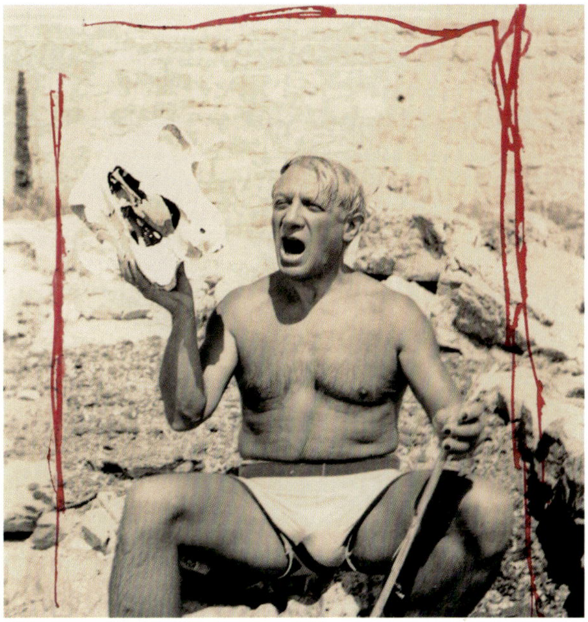

Picasso as Minotaur, Mougins, 1937, by Dora Maar

The fall of Madrid after fierce fighting in spring 1939 would be transposed by the artist in the allegorical canvas *Chat saisissant un oiseau* (*Cat Catching a Bird*), which encapsulates the demise of the young Republic and Franco's victory.

At the same time, the large-sized "cartoon" for a tapestry, *Femmes à leur toilette* (*Women in the Bathroom*, 1937–38), conjures the hedonistic theme of the harem or Turkish bath. The wallpapers comprising it were used by Picasso in 1937 to check against the tones of gray in *Guernica*, as is revealed by the photographs of the work taken by Dora Maar during its execution. *Women in the Bathroom* thus appears as a "positive" of the picture in grisaille—its polychrome doppelgänger, in which female figures are exalted as symbols of life and hope. The cartoon also scaled up the formal and spatial resources of collage (as experimented with in *Nature morte à la chaise cannée* [*Still Life with Cane Chair*] and the papiers collés of 1912–14), a principle that had continued to irrigate Picasso's output since the cubist period.

A series of portraits dated 1937–39 was a deliberate tribute to Van Gogh, whose oeuvre, lambasted by the Nazis as "degenerate art," was being publicly burned in Berlin. Borrowing his attire, as well as his color scheme and expressionistic virulence, in *Homme au chapeau de paille et au cornet de glace* (*Man with a Straw Hat and an Ice Cream Cone*, 1938), Picasso produced a self-portrait in Van Gogh's features. Likewise, Picasso imposed the master's stylistic idiom on contemporary portraits of Marie-Thérèse Walter and Dora Maar, which display chromatic tracery and a scarified palette. Informed by the geometrical faces of the protocubism of *Les Demoiselles d'Avignon*, the angelic features of his lovers are deformed through the deconstructive prism of a revived cubist method.

Hunkered down in Royan by the time war was declared in September 1939, Picasso painted many portraits of nameless, unseeing women, wearing plaited straw hats and with faces swollen into blocks, who materialize the enigmatic variation of generic portraiture: paintings of war, masks of death, the faces of the maimed. These figures synthesized the visionary identity of painting on the eve of the bloodshed about to engulf the world.

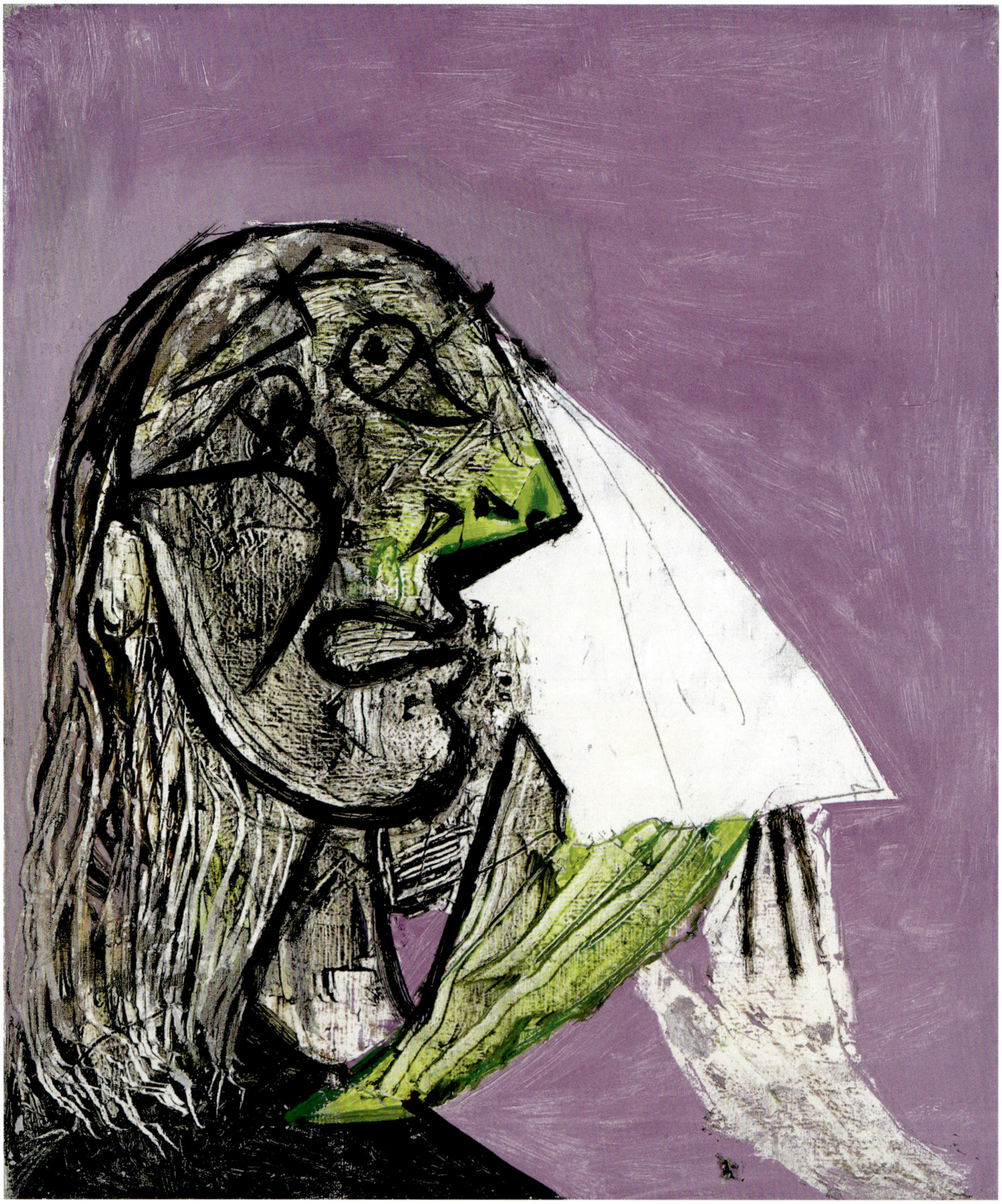

 The Weeping Woman, October 18, 1937

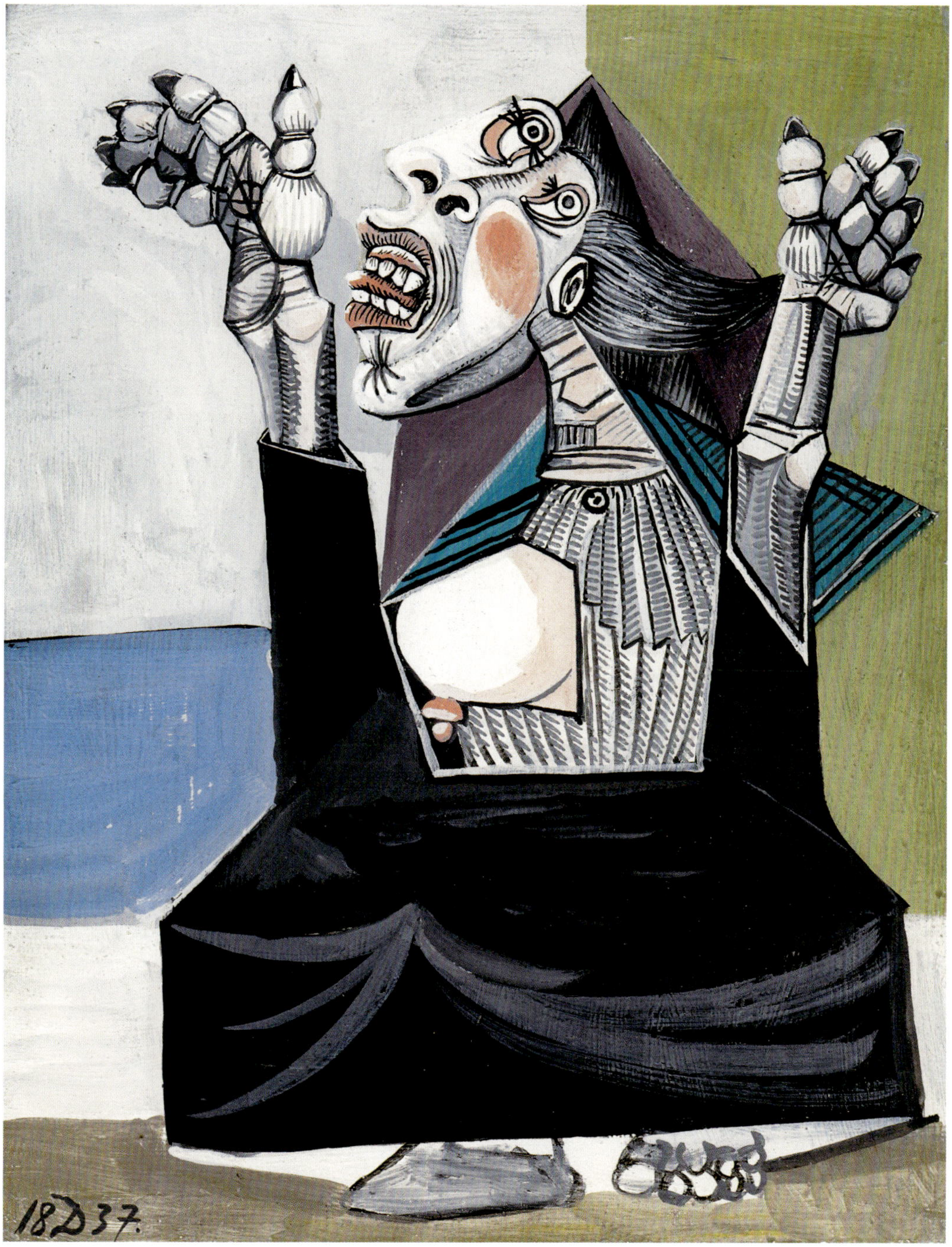

The Suppliant, December 18, 1937

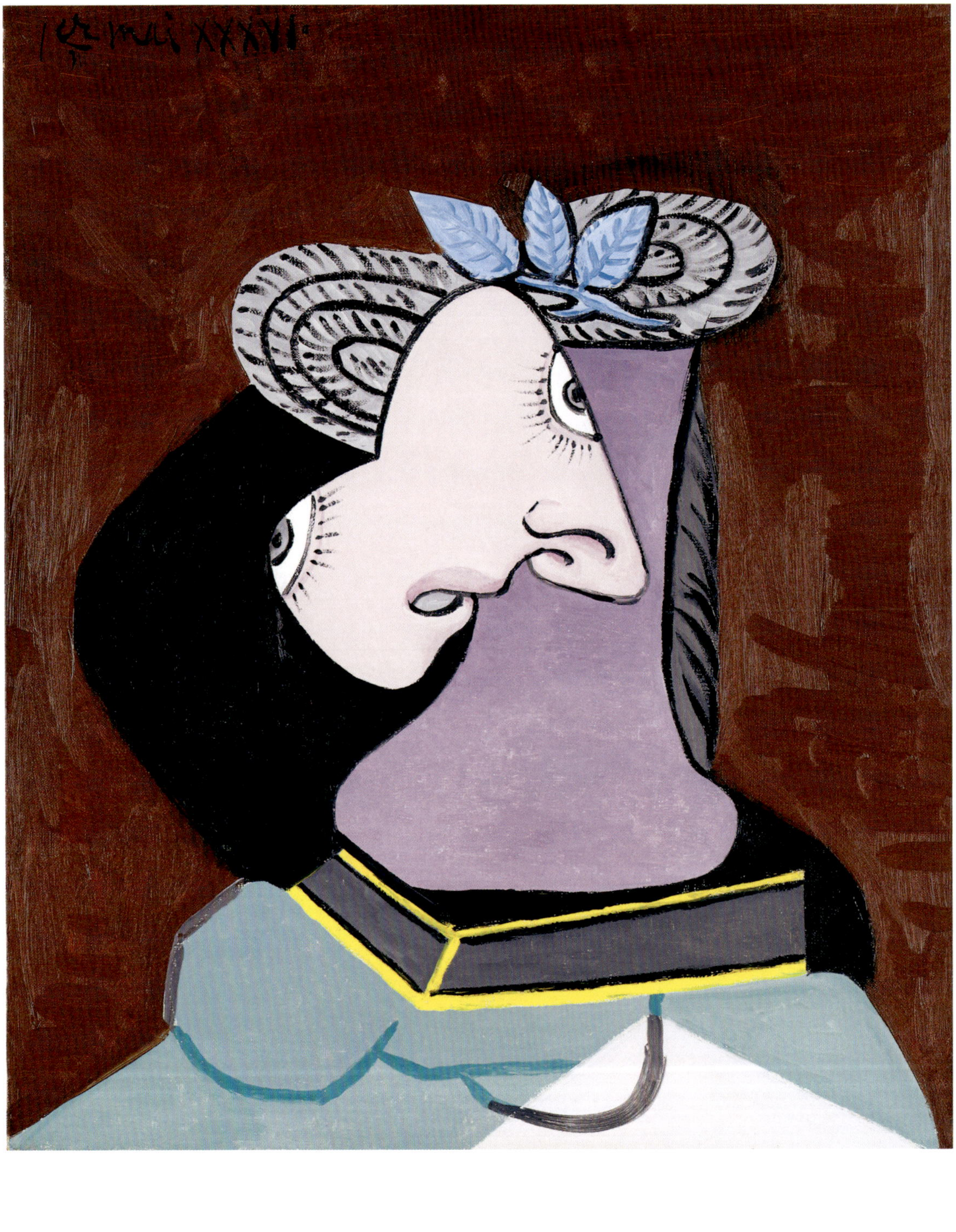

62 *The Straw Hat with Blue Leaves*, May 1, 1936

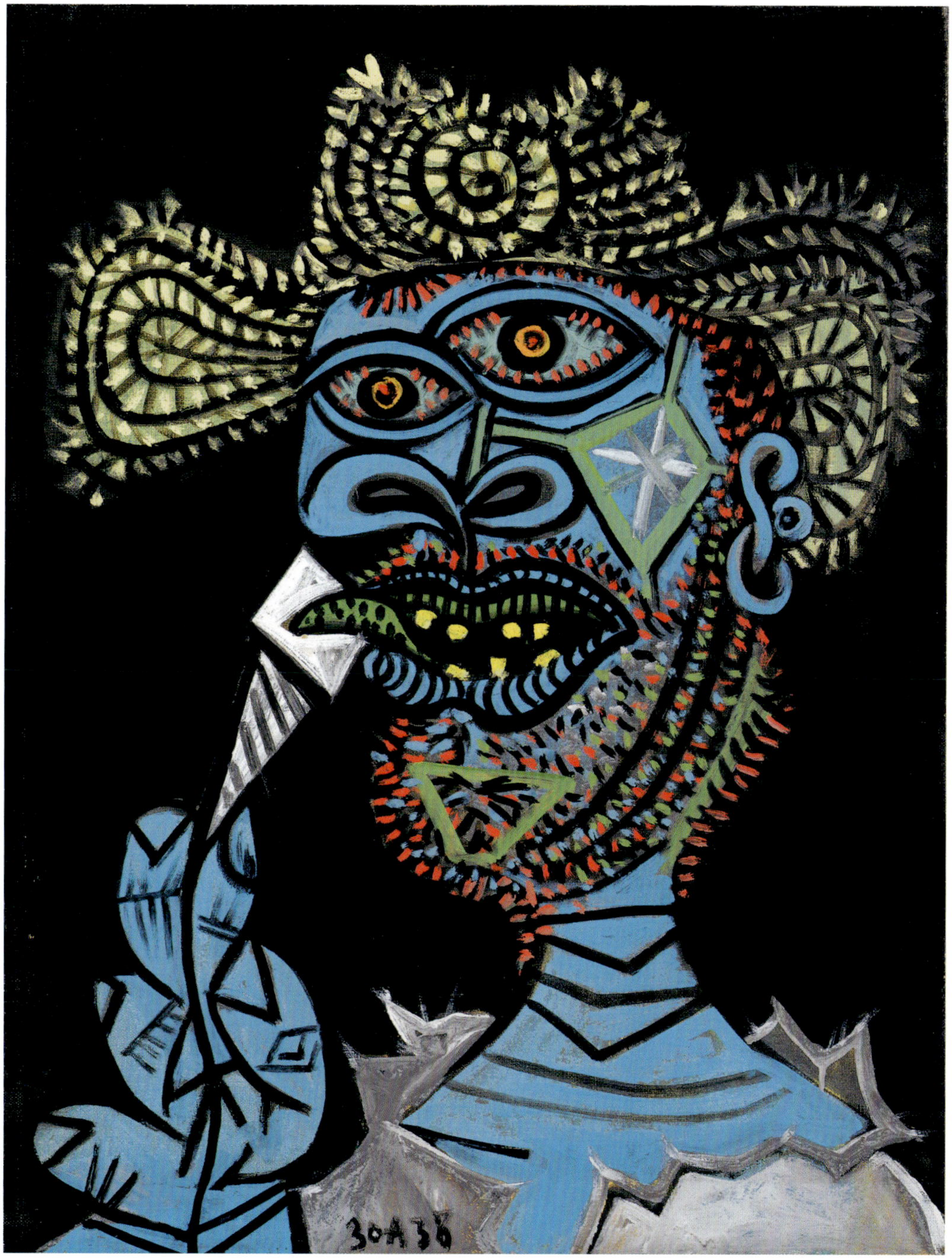

Man with a Straw Hat and an Ice Cream Cone, August 30, 1938

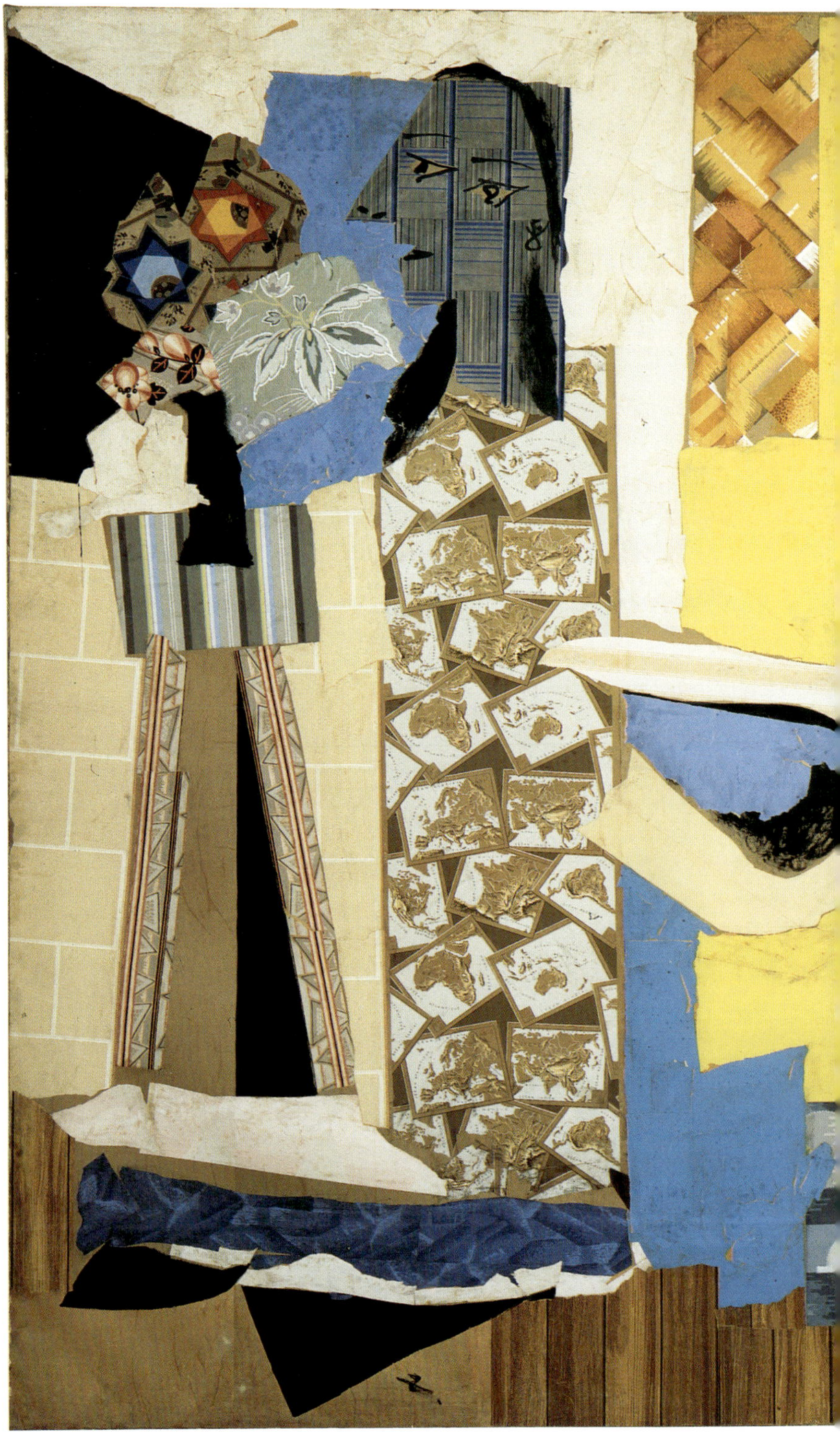

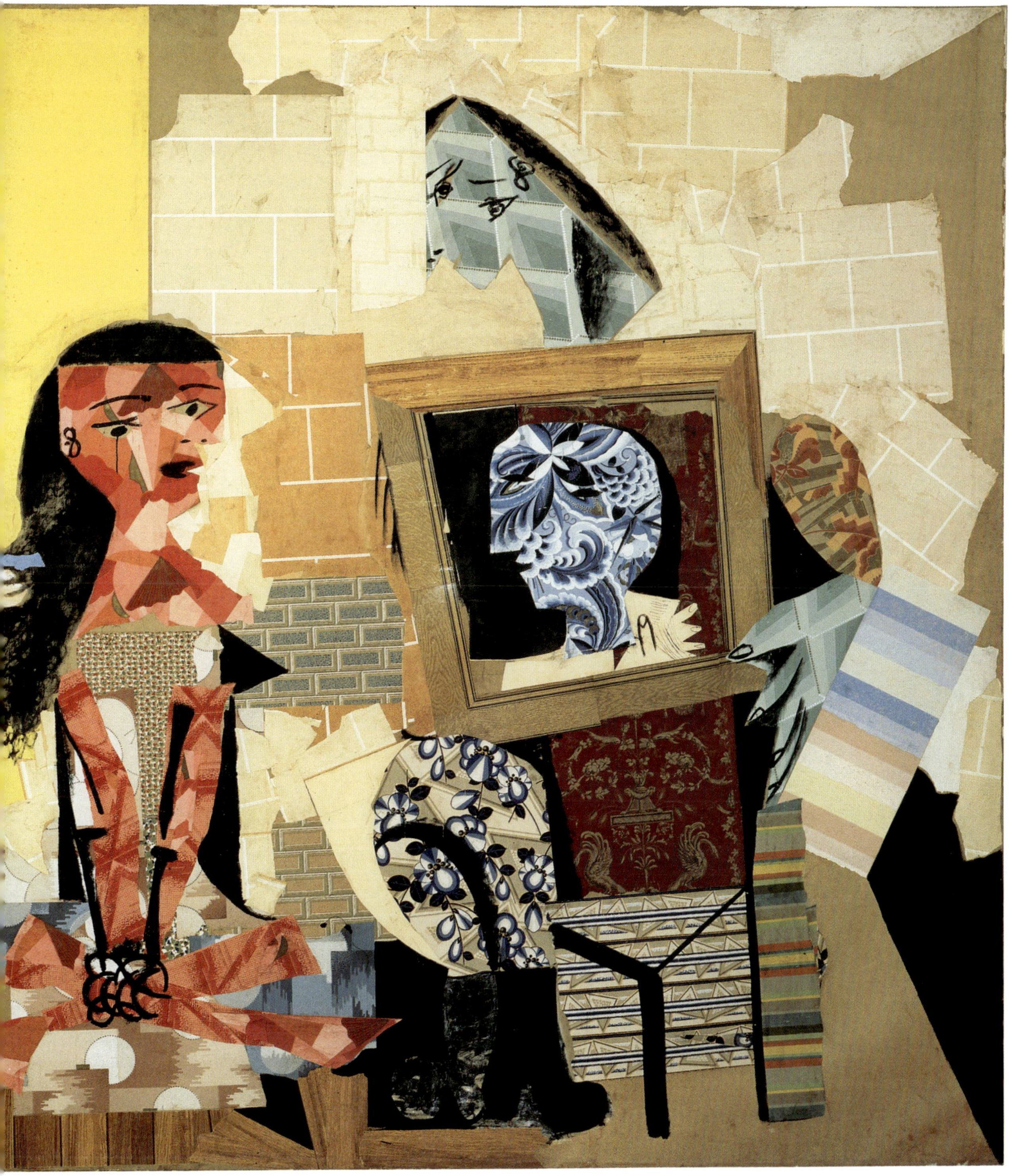

Women in the Bathroom, winter 1937–38

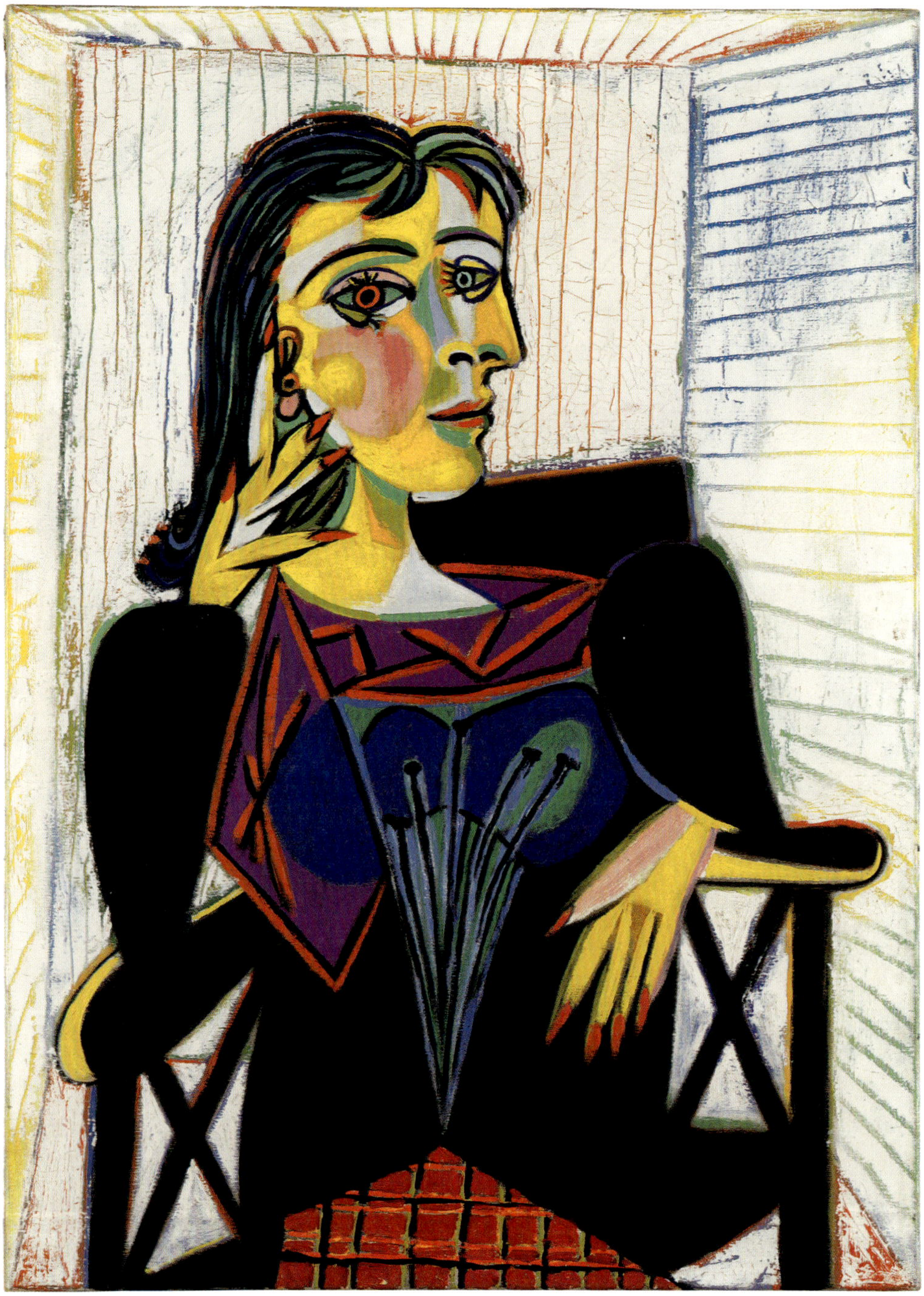

 Portrait of Dora Maar, 1937

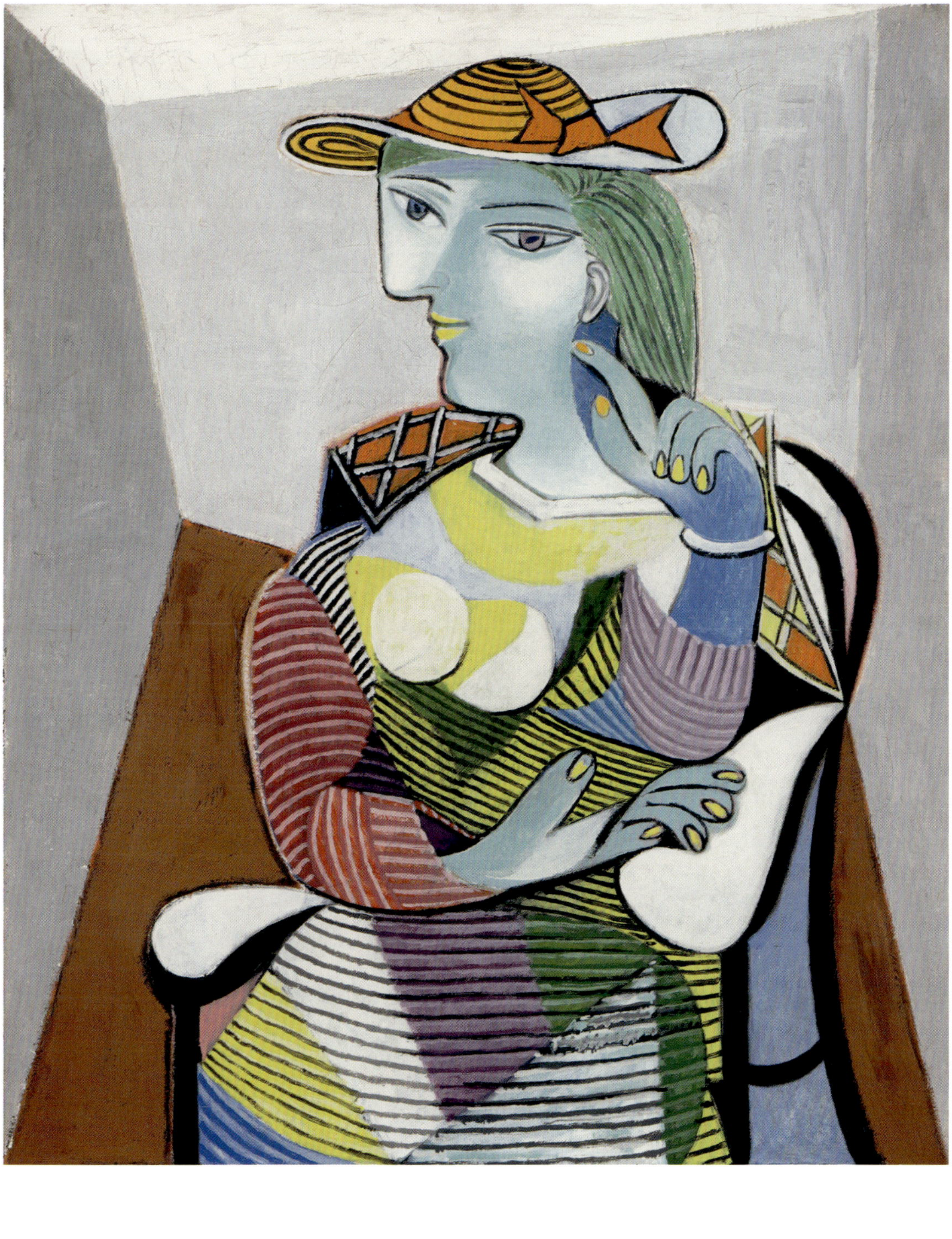

Portrait of Marie-Thérèse, January 6, 1937

1940
1945

"Painting … is a tool
of offensive and defensive war
against the enemy."

Pablo Picasso, in Simone Téry, interview with Picasso, *Les Lettres françaises*, Paris, March 24, 1945

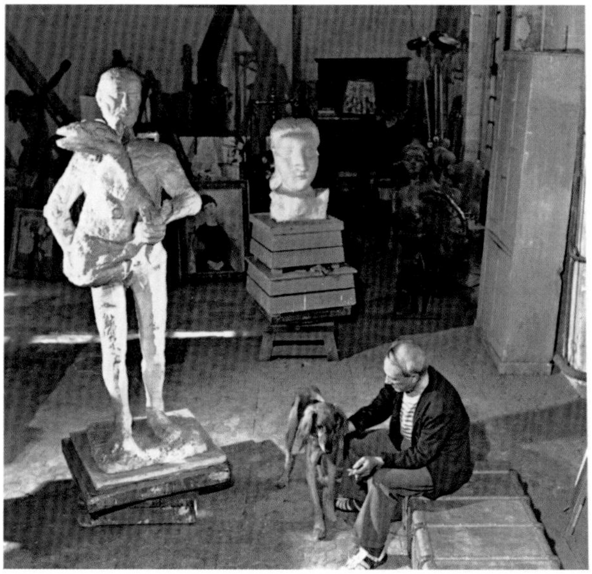

Picasso in his studio with *Man with a Sheep*, Grands-Augustins studio, c. 1944, by Robert Capa

During the early months of World War II, in an effort to articulate the searing drama then tearing Europe apart, Picasso painted death itself with the enigmatic features of a Dora Maar skinned alive. At the end of August 1940, he returned to Paris, to rue des Grands-Augustins, where he remained until the Liberation.

Christian Zervos contradicted the two symmetrical myths of the artist, as either having benefited from the best of arrangements with the occupying authorities, or else having been an active member of the Resistance, when he wrote: "During the Occupation, Picasso simply kept his dignity, as did millions of other people. It should be understood that the work itself is the highest form of resistance."

It was a time when some Parisian artists traveled to Germany at the invitation of the Propagandastaffel, among them onetime "Fauves," such as Kees Van Dongen, Maurice de Vlaminck, and André Derain. In April 1942, Vlaminck launched a violent attack on Picasso in the columns of a literary review, *Comoedia*. Forbidden to exhibit or publish, under surveillance by the Gestapo, and threatened in 1941 with extradition to Spain, where Franco had demanded his head, Picasso withdrew to his studio, the windows blacked out, to reinvent his oeuvre.

In the heat of the crusade against "degenerate art"—whose symbol Picasso had become—he used pages from the collaborationist newspaper, *Paris-Soir*, as a palette and support, to paint studies, outlines of heads, hands, and feet in black, which blazed a trail for the great emblematic canvases of the period. Obliterating or doctoring illustrations from the press, he protested against lies and misinformation. *Tête de femme* (*Head of a Woman*, 1941), traced in black on newsprint—a geometrical effigy that heralds the bronze *Tête de mort* (*Death's Head*) of 1943—established itself as a protest against indignity. *Tête de mort*: "a huge petrified head with empty eye-sockets... like a block of wandering stone, gouged out into cavities, corroded and polished with having spent so long rolling from age to age," like *L'Homme au mouton* (*Man with a Sheep*, 1943), express their fossil-like and archaic nature (Brassaï, *Conversations with Picasso*, 1964).

Confronted with the cult of brute force preached by Nazism, Picasso endeavored to celebrate both the domestic world as well as underlying, unconscious forms, as much of sexuality as of undifferentiated vital drive. *Jeune garçon à la langouste* (*Boy with a Crayfish*, 1941), *L'Enfant aux colombes* (*The Child with Doves*, 1943), and *Le Chat* (*The Cat*, 1943) thus drew up an inventory of a private world, borrowing their power from a poetically dream-like fantasy. These hieratic figures of children and animals formed the emblems, the coats of arms, for a visceral, inborn resistance to all forms of domination and indoctrination.

Emblematic of the war period, the vast canvas *Le Charnier* (*The Charnel House*, 1945, Museum of Modern Art, New York) garnered a lukewarm reception from the French Communist Party, which the painter had recently joined in October 1944, and which was then, more than ever, promoting the Zhdanovian principle of socialist realism. However, Picasso refused to submit to it and to limit his art solely to the role of documentation or to militant tub-thumping. "I did not paint the war because I am not one of those painters, who, like a photographer, sets off in search of a subject. Still, there can be no doubt that the war exists in the pictures I made at the time." (Jean Leymarie, *Picasso, métamorphoses et unité*, 1971).

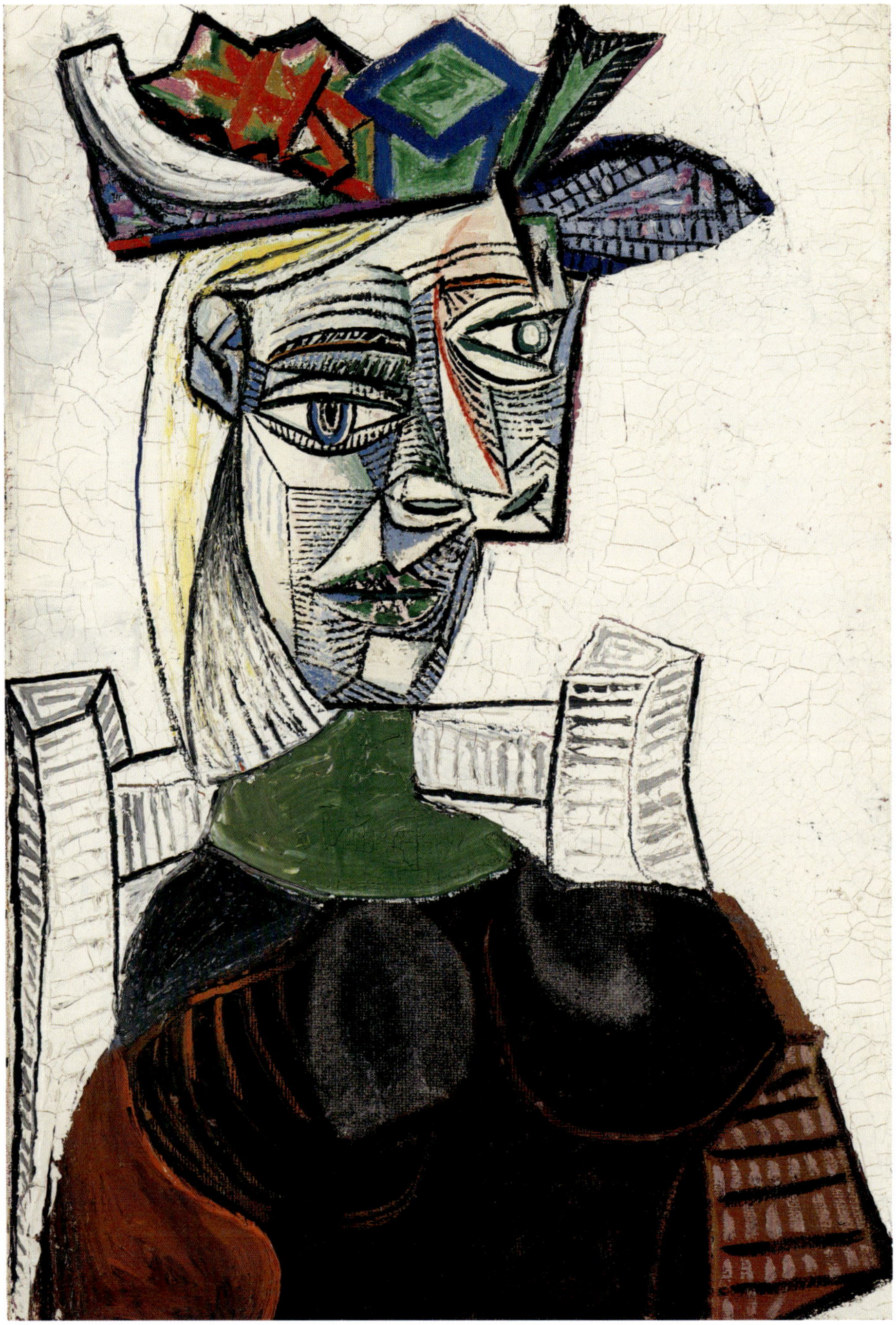

 Seated Woman with a Hat, May 27, 1939

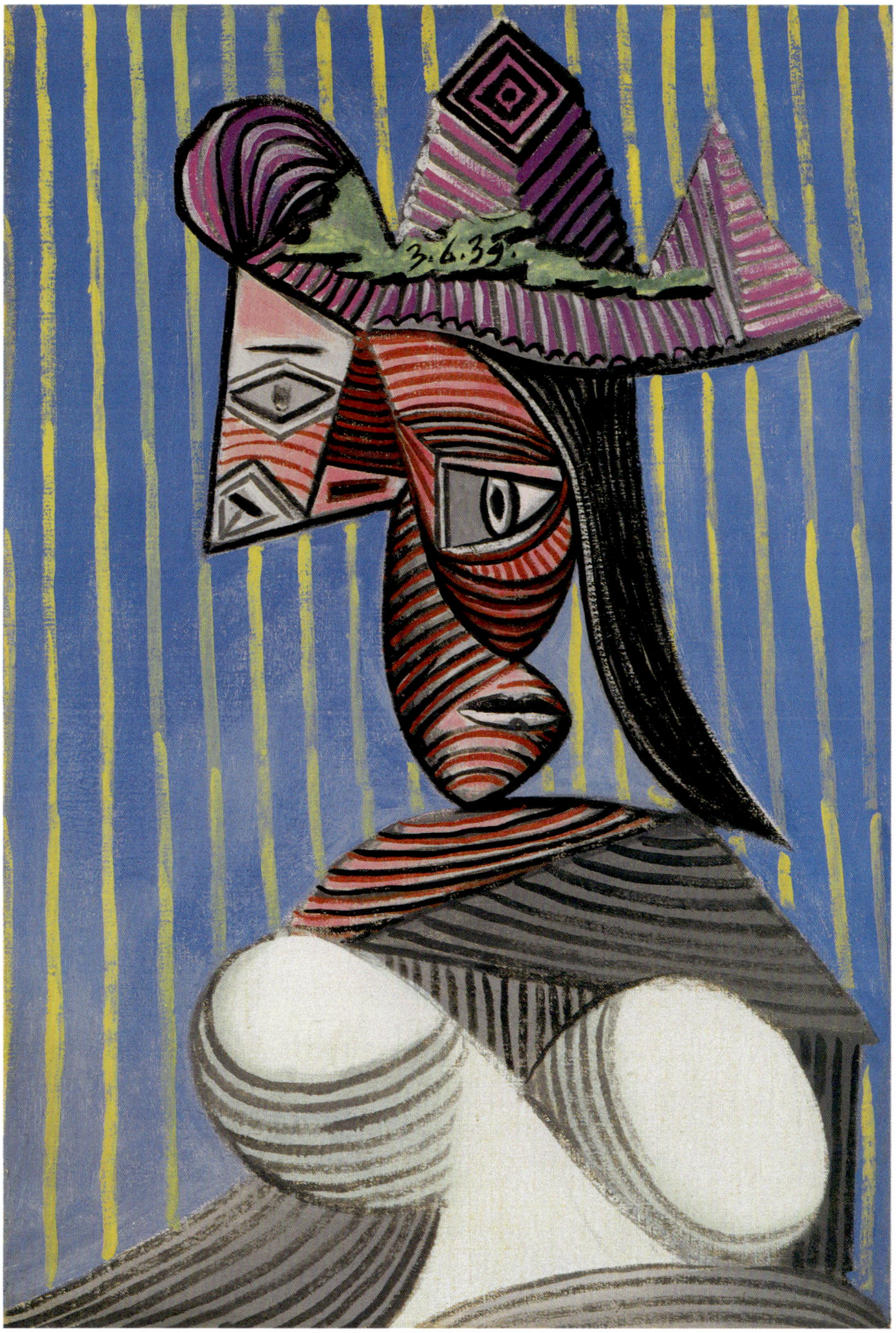

Bust of Woman with a Striped Hat, June 3, 1939

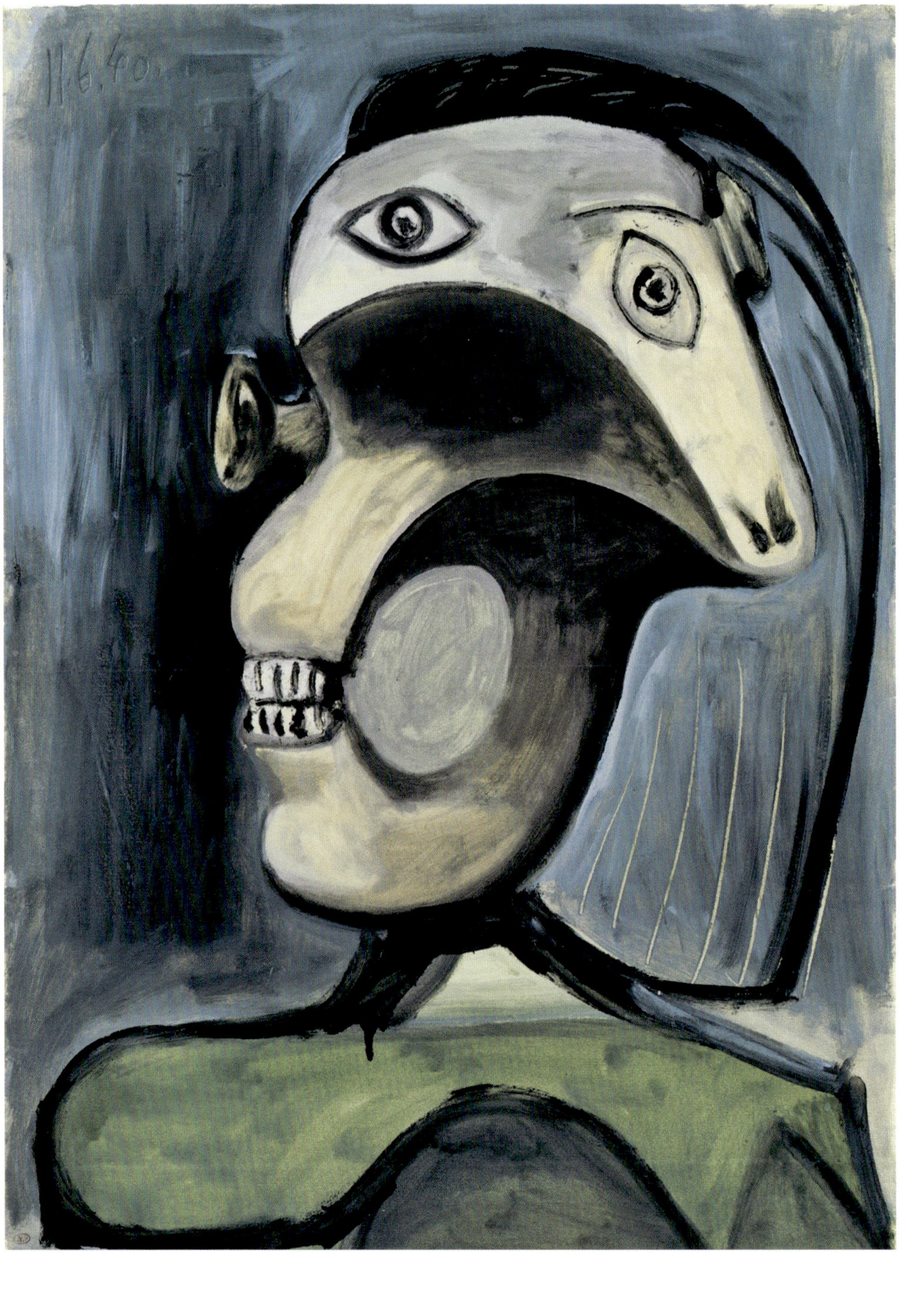

 Head of a Woman, June 11, 1940

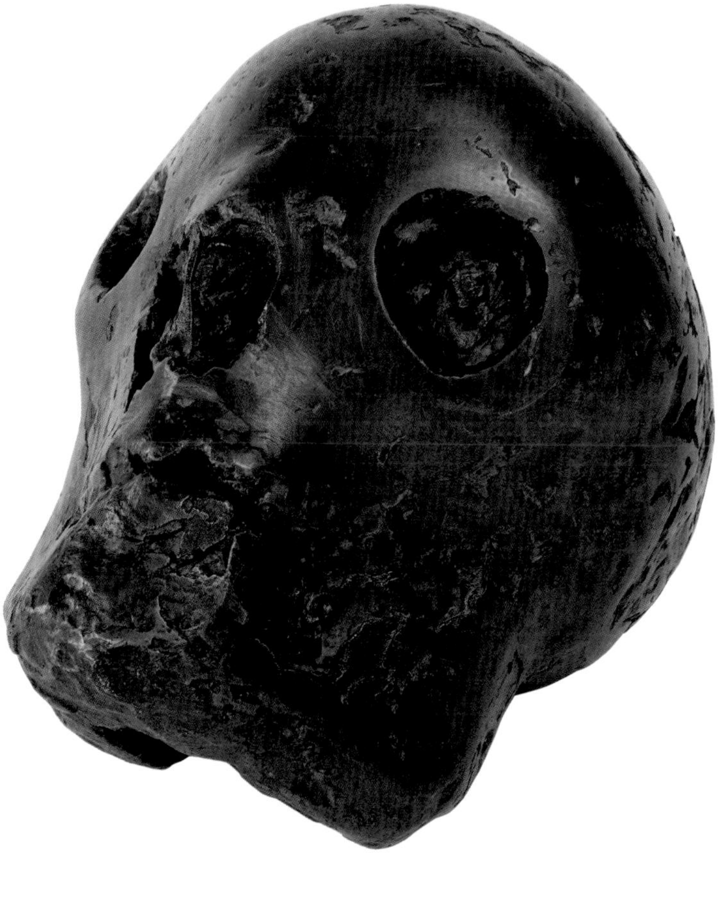

Death's Head, 1943

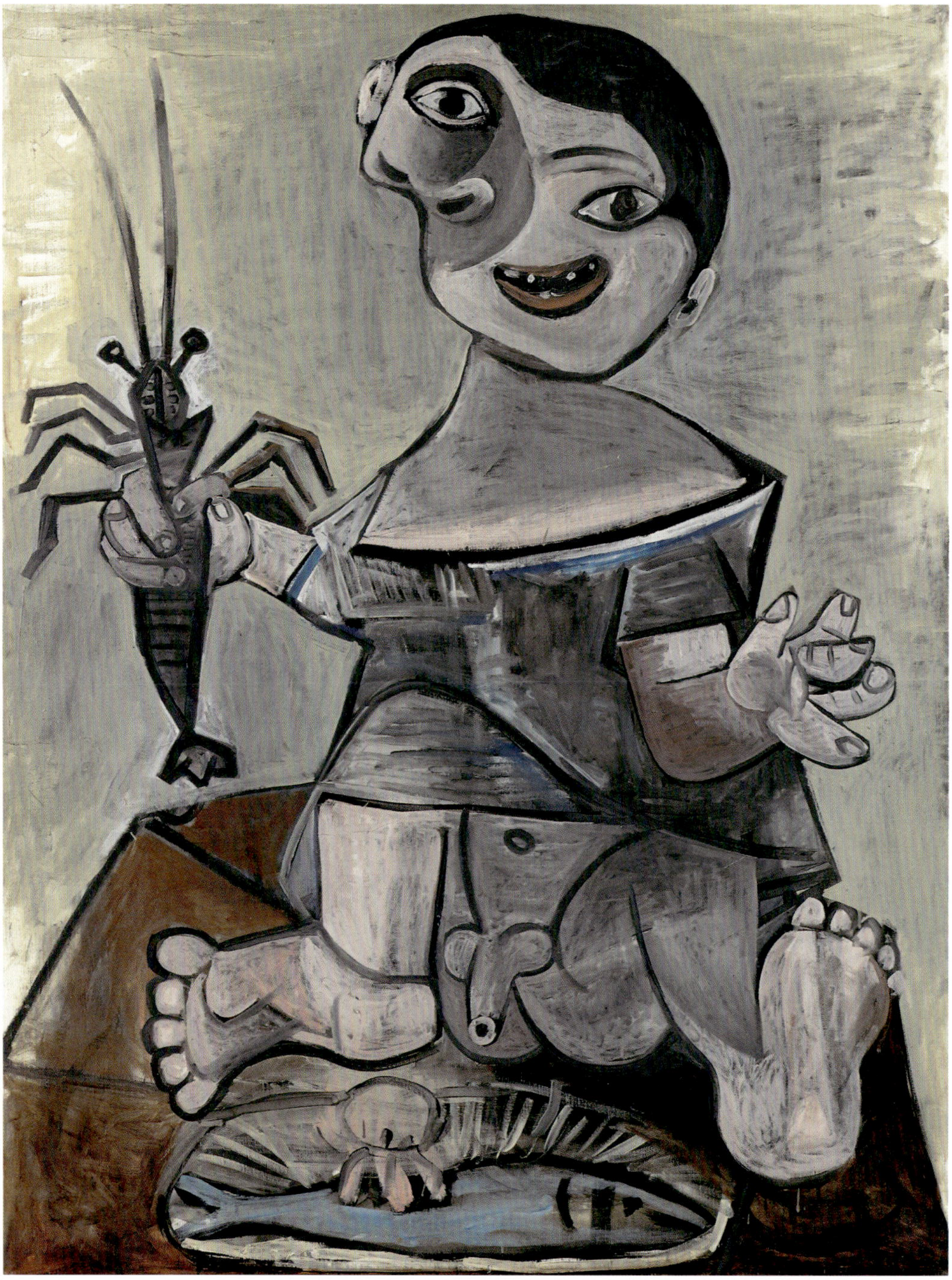

 Boy with a Crayfish, June 21, 1941

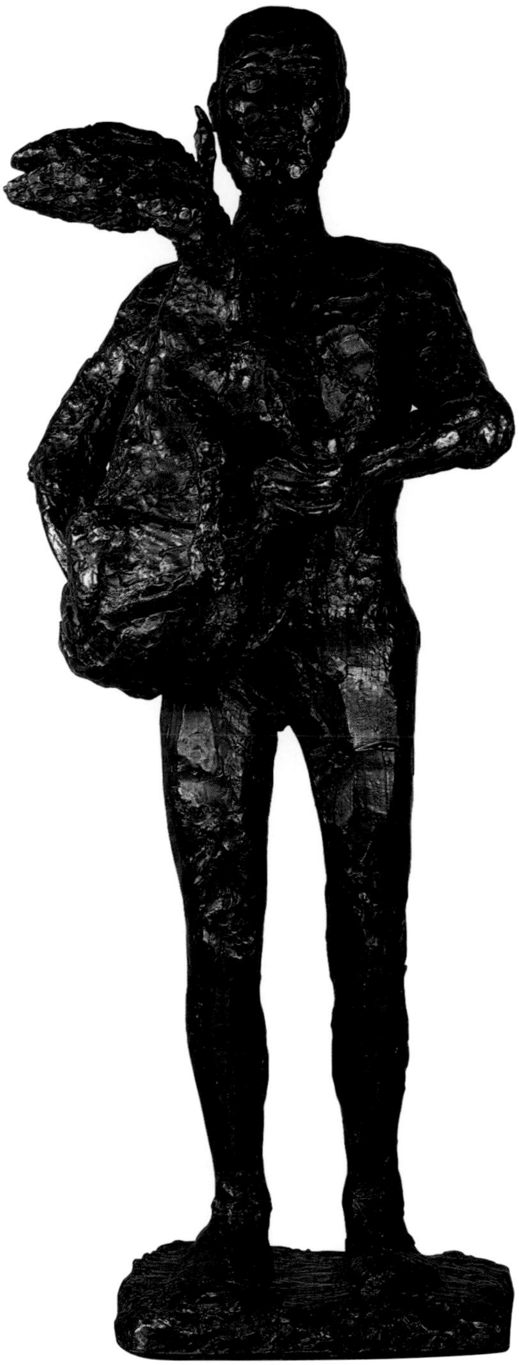

Man with a Sheep, February 1943

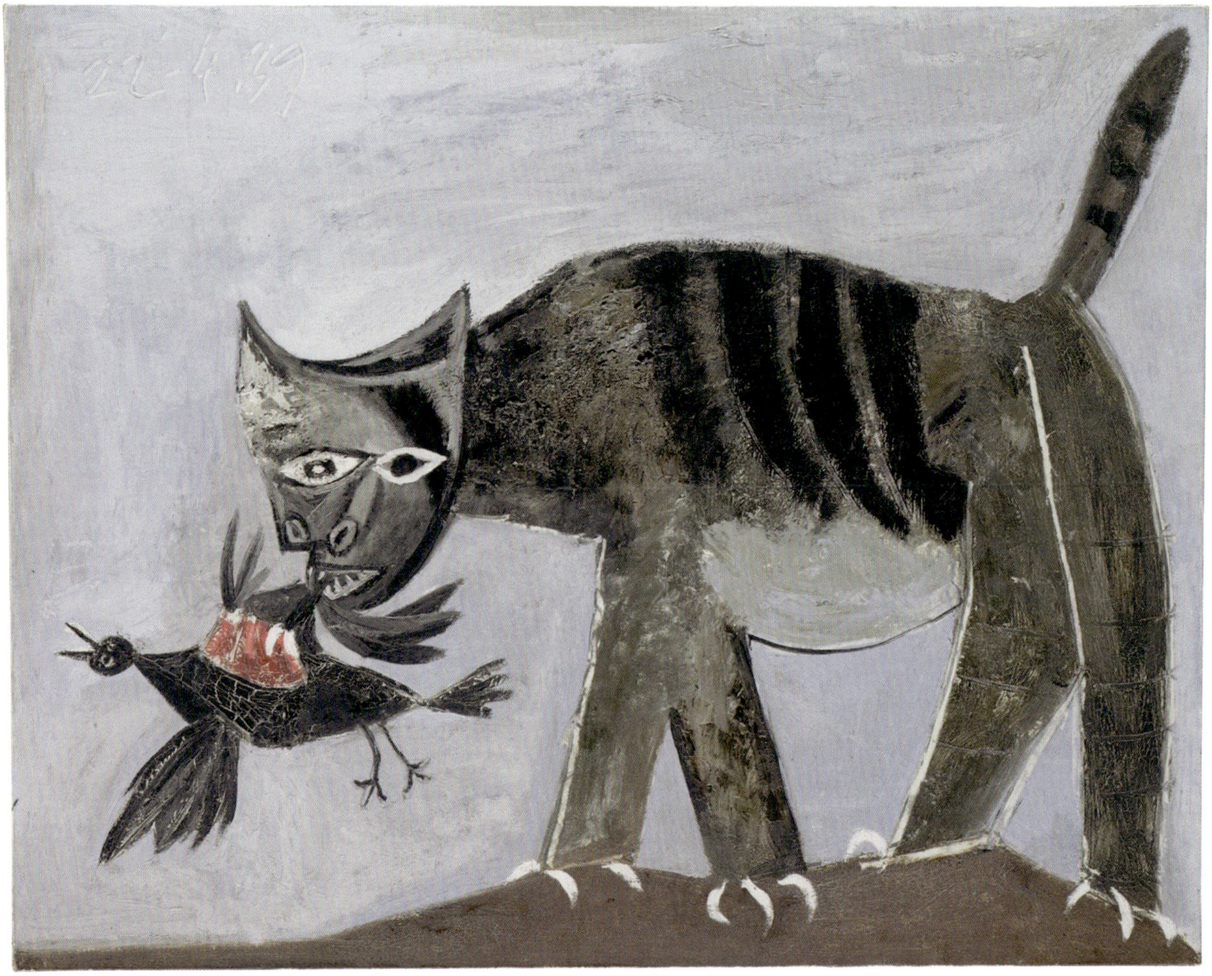

 Cat Catching a Bird, April 22, 1939

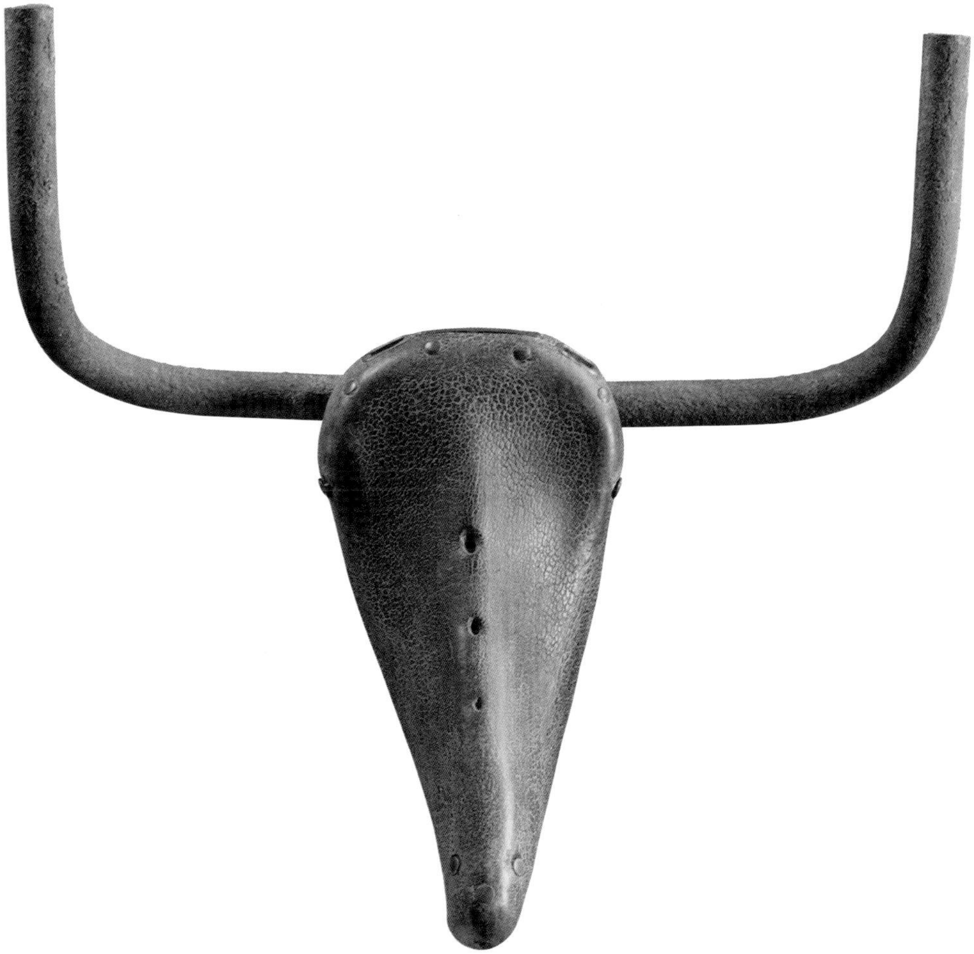

Head of a Bull, spring 1942

1946
1960

"The artist is a receptacle for emotions that come from all over the place: from the sky, from the earth, from a scrap of paper, from a passing shape, from a spider's web."

Pablo Picasso, in Christian Zervos, "Conversations avec Picasso," *Cahiers d'Art* (special edition, 1935)

In 1946, Picasso settled with the young painter Françoise Gilot in Vallauris, a potters' village in the south of France. As a member of the Communist Party from autumn 1944, Picasso saw himself as a "worker painter," a "militant artist." The artist attempted to put the democratization of art into practice by multiplying the artistic gesture. He wanted to relativize the concept of the original, of the uniqueness of the artwork, to throw open the doors of art to the world at large. His work as a ceramist numbers nearly six hundred pieces and variants in all (a hundred or so pieces are part of the museum's collection), all carried out in collaboration with potters in the Madoura pottery. In the same vein, posters printed from large linocuts spawned rich and intriguing visual inventions, in a vast number of proofs that place the concept of variation at the center of his oeuvre. Deriving their subject matter from popular imagery, Picasso's ceramics and linocuts portray nearby localities typical of the region, such as the Nerolium, a distillery where orange-flower essence, or neroli, is still produced. In his canvases the artist delineates the world of the craftsmen in Vallauris, living amid the toxic smoke from the kilns, in a Mediterranean world already under the threat of urban sprawl and the mass tourism that—from the 1960s—imposed itself as the Côte d'Azur's chief economic activity.

From 1946 to 1953, working out of his studio, the Atelier du Fournas, Picasso conjured up new metamorphoses based on found objects. Each morning, on his way to the studio from his little village house, La Galloise, he would collect material for sculptures from ditches, fields, and wasteland. Assembling these finds into collages and composite montages that hover between two worlds, Picasso applied surrealist procedures to the precarious postwar economy: baskets, lead piping, chipped vases, branches, firedogs, a kiln tile, cake molds, household refuse, and industrial and artisanal detritus are just some of the materials that make up these pieces. *Petite fille sautant à la corde* (*Little Girl Skipping*, 1952), *La Chèvre* (*The Goat*, 1950), *La Femme à la poussette* (*Woman with a Pushchair*, 1950), *L'Arrosoir fleuri* (*The Flowering Watering Can*, 1951–52) form a sequence of large sculptures carried out by Picasso in accordance with this eminently poetic principle, by which the eye can synthesize every object into a fascinating reinvention. Due to its ductile character, plaster is able to link and fuse disparate elements of reality into new semantic entities. Delighted to rediscover in these works the subversive vein of Picasso's 1930s work, Jean Cocteau paid the following tribute: "You are a ragman and a handyman of genius." The virtuoso series of composite plasters, *La Grue* (*The Crane*, 1951), *La Petite Chouette* (*The Little Owl*, 1951), *La Guenon et son petit* (*Baboon with its Young*, 1951) are each episodes in the transformation of the everyday into a new hybrid bestiary of minor household gods. Soon, the birth of his children Claude and Paloma—with *La Femme enceinte* (*The Pregnant Woman*, 1949) celebrating the event—was having its own effect on the process of recreating new rules: play, toys, and replicas are tools in a manipulation of the mundane and the prosaic into a brutalist, playful representation of the world.

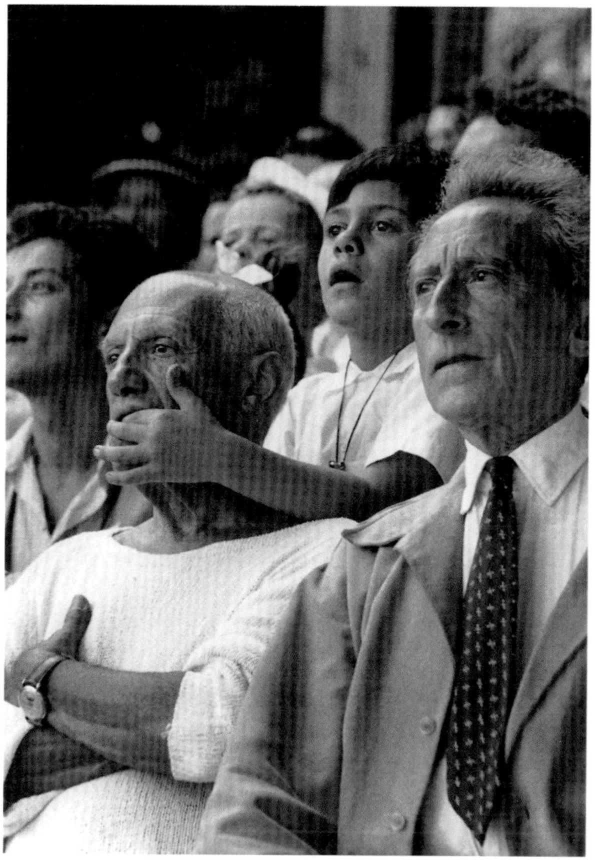

Picasso, Jean Cocteau, and Claude at the bullfight, Vallauris, 1955, by Brian Brake

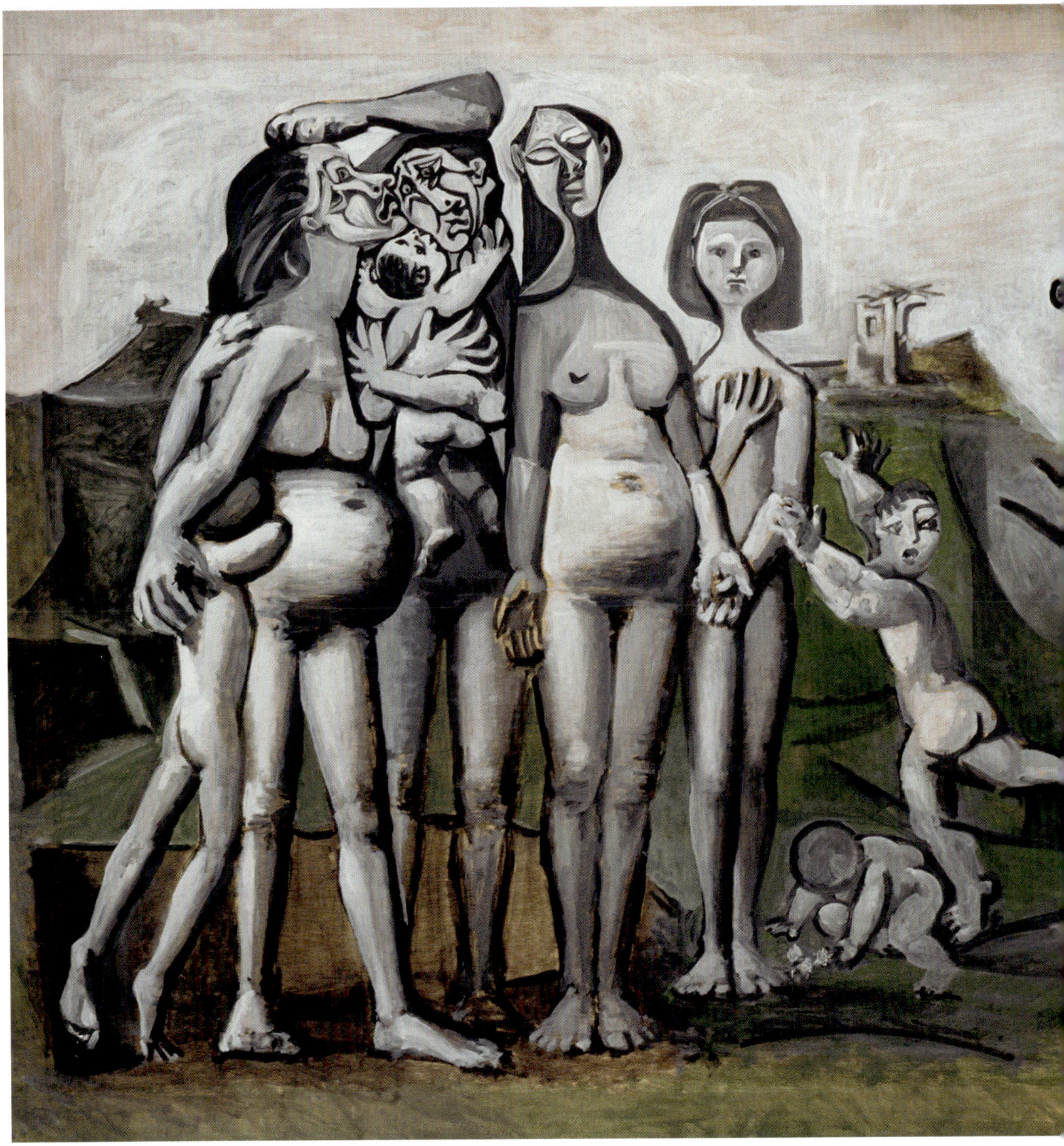

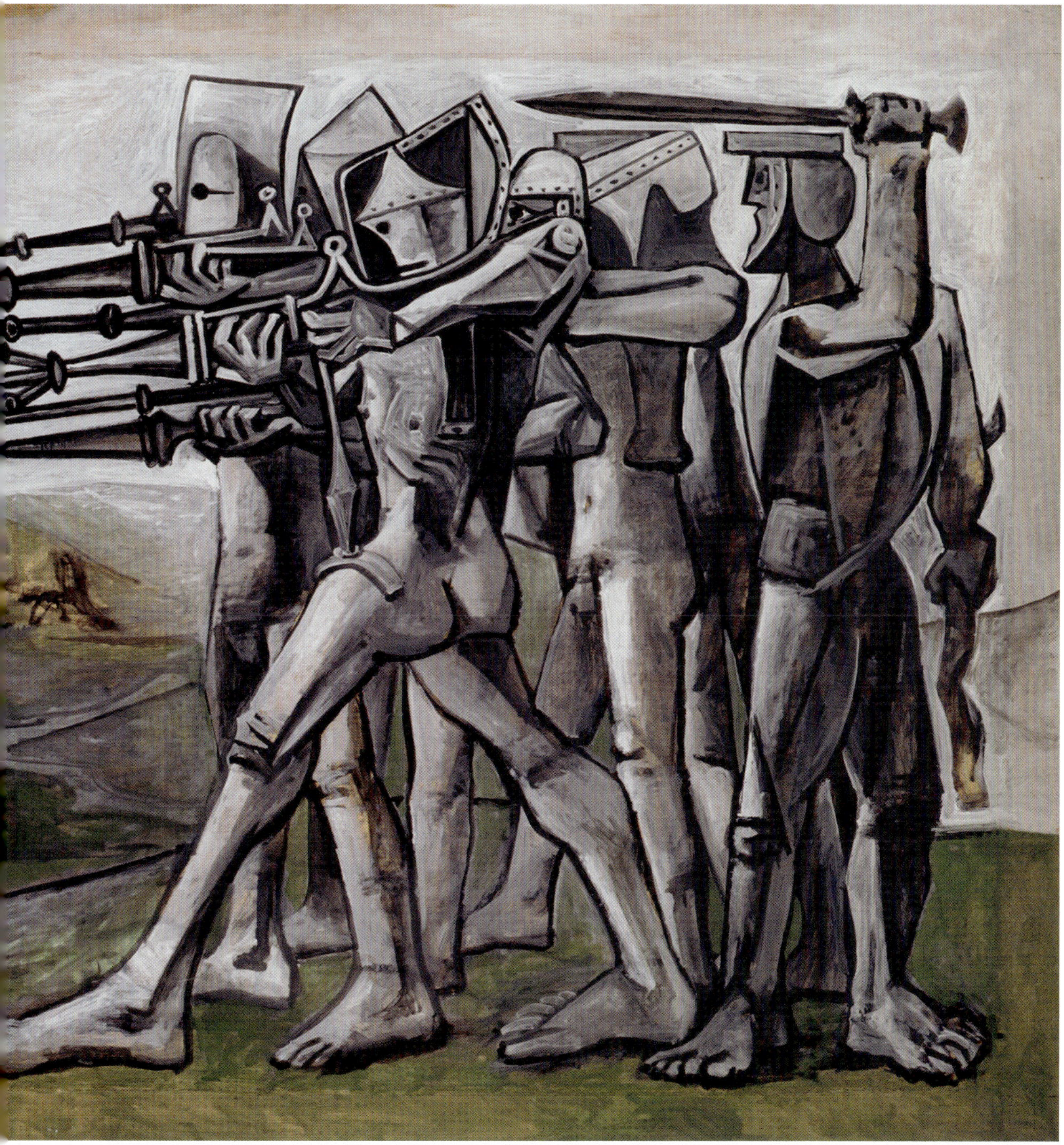

Massacre in Korea, January 18, 1951

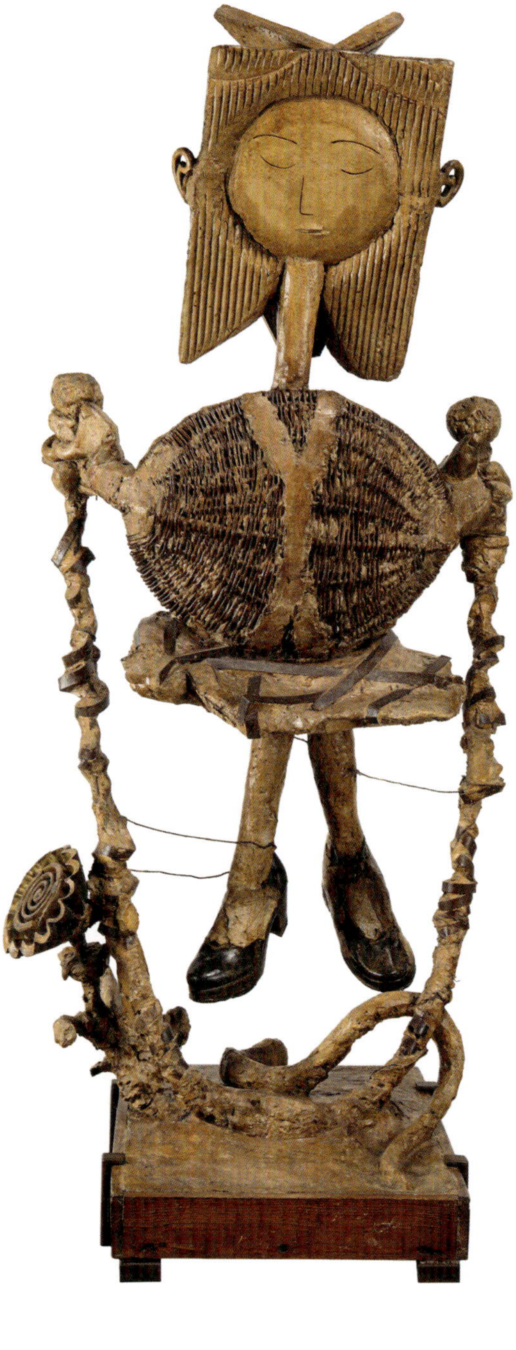

 Little Girl Skipping, 1952

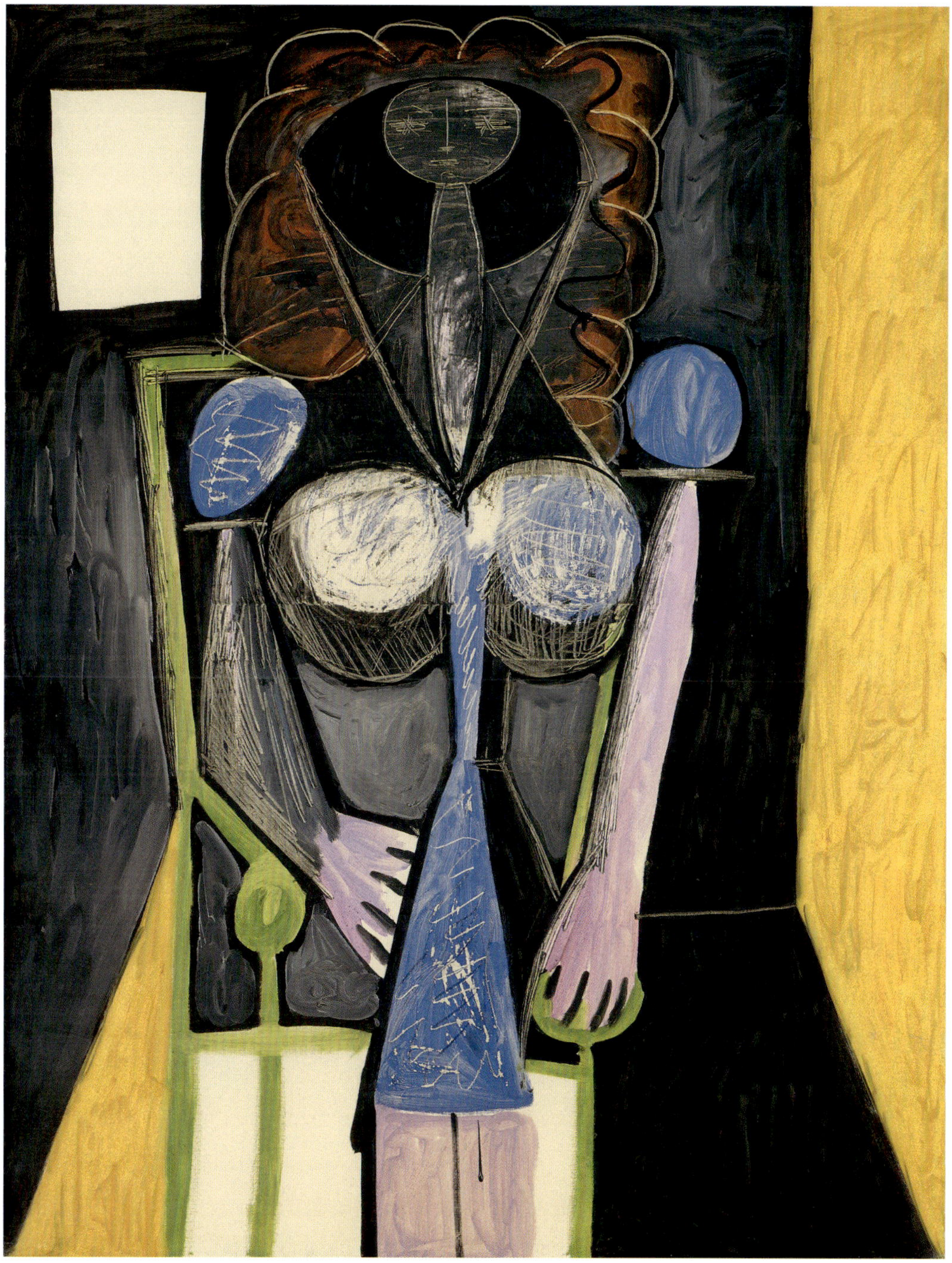

Woman in an Armchair, July 3, 1946

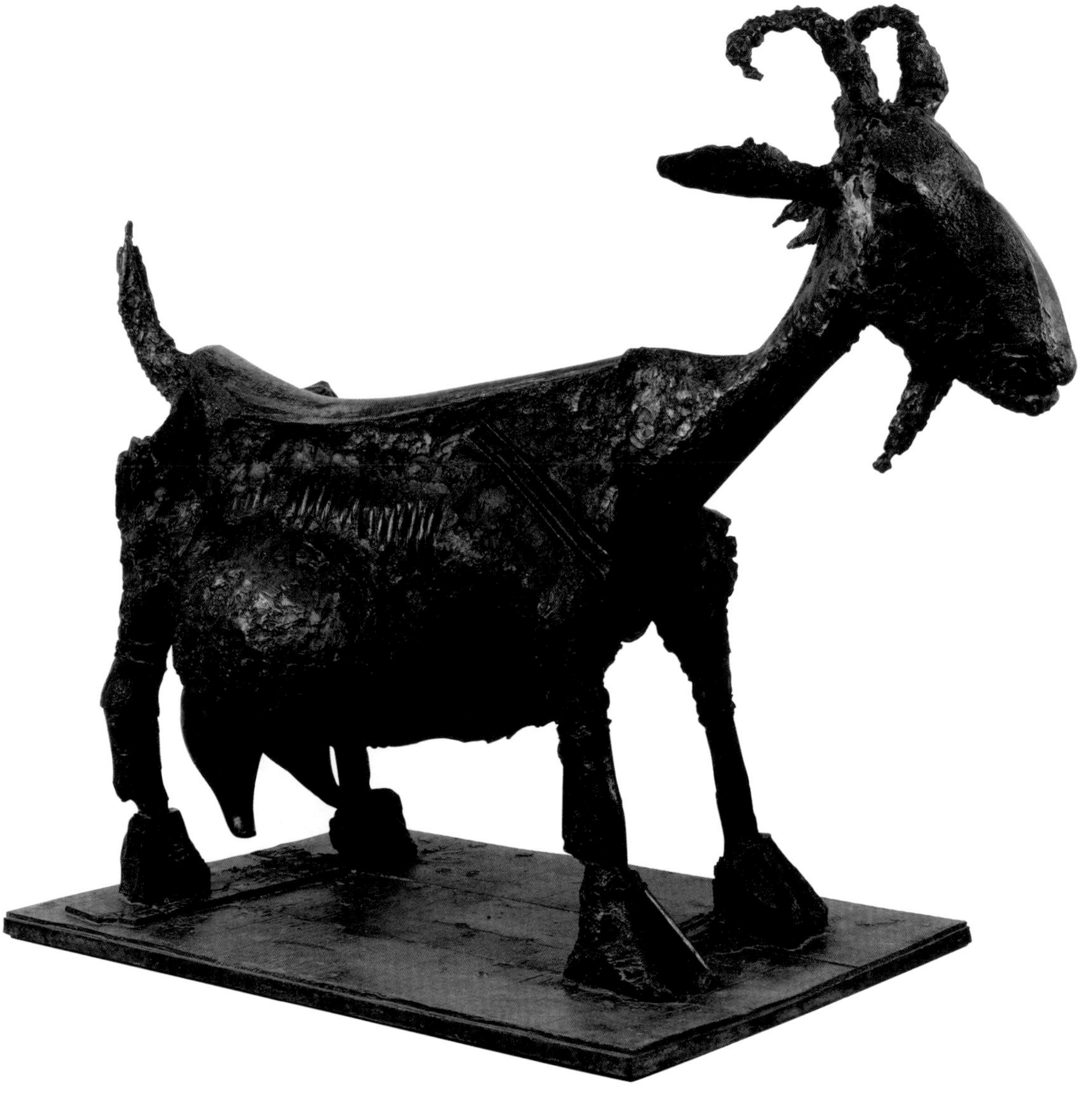

 The Goat, 1950

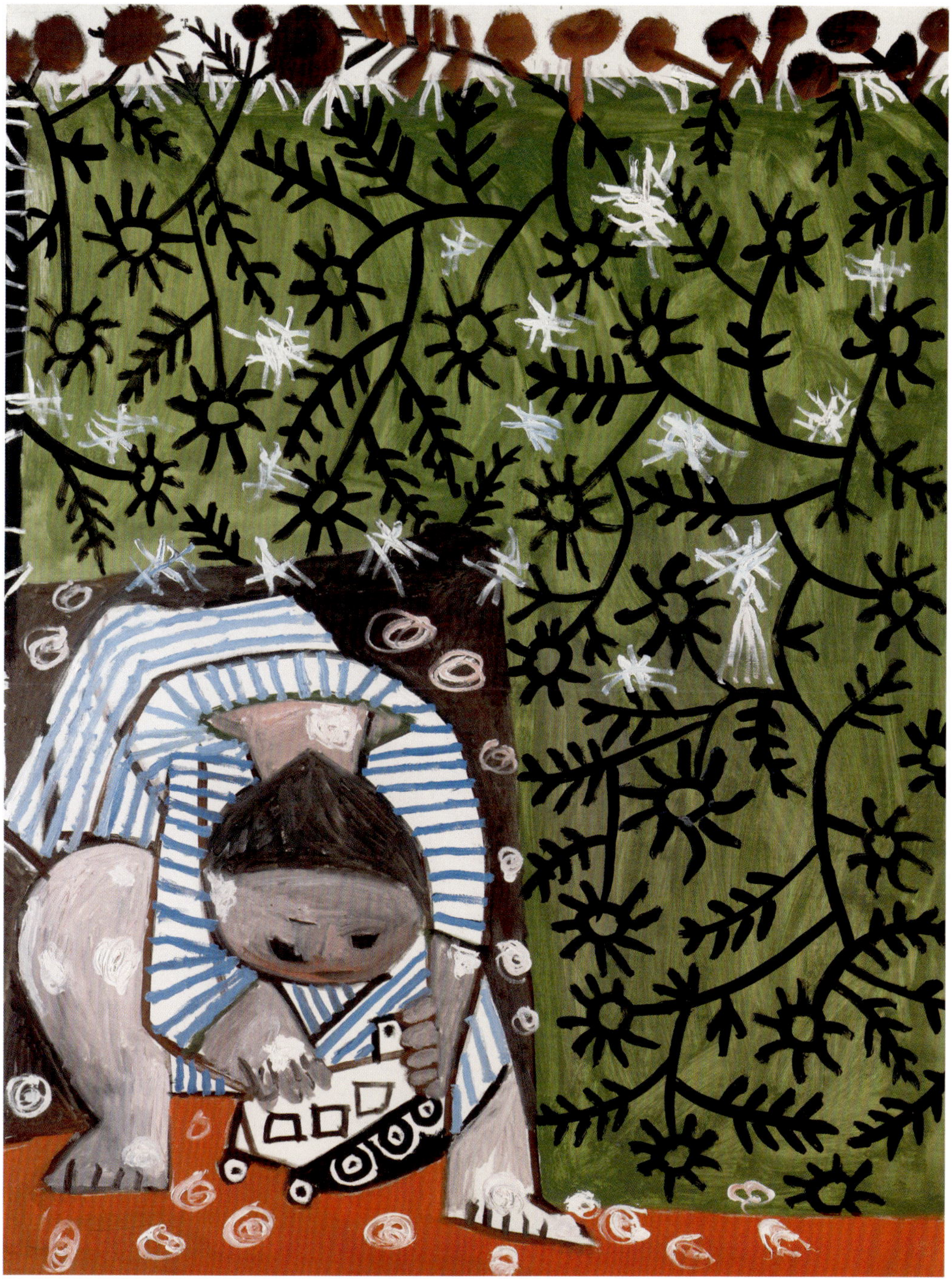

Child Playing with a Toy Truck, December 27, 1953

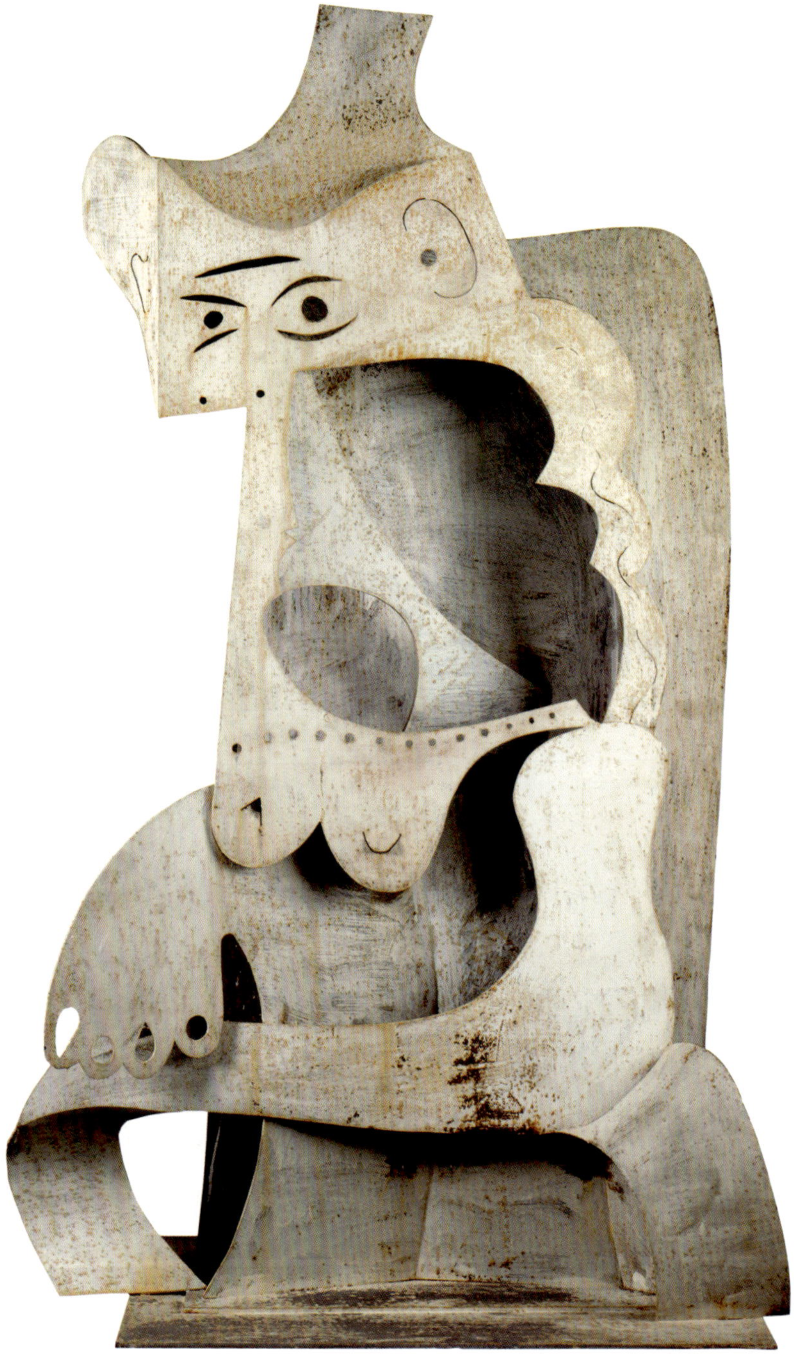

86 *Woman in a Hat*, 1961

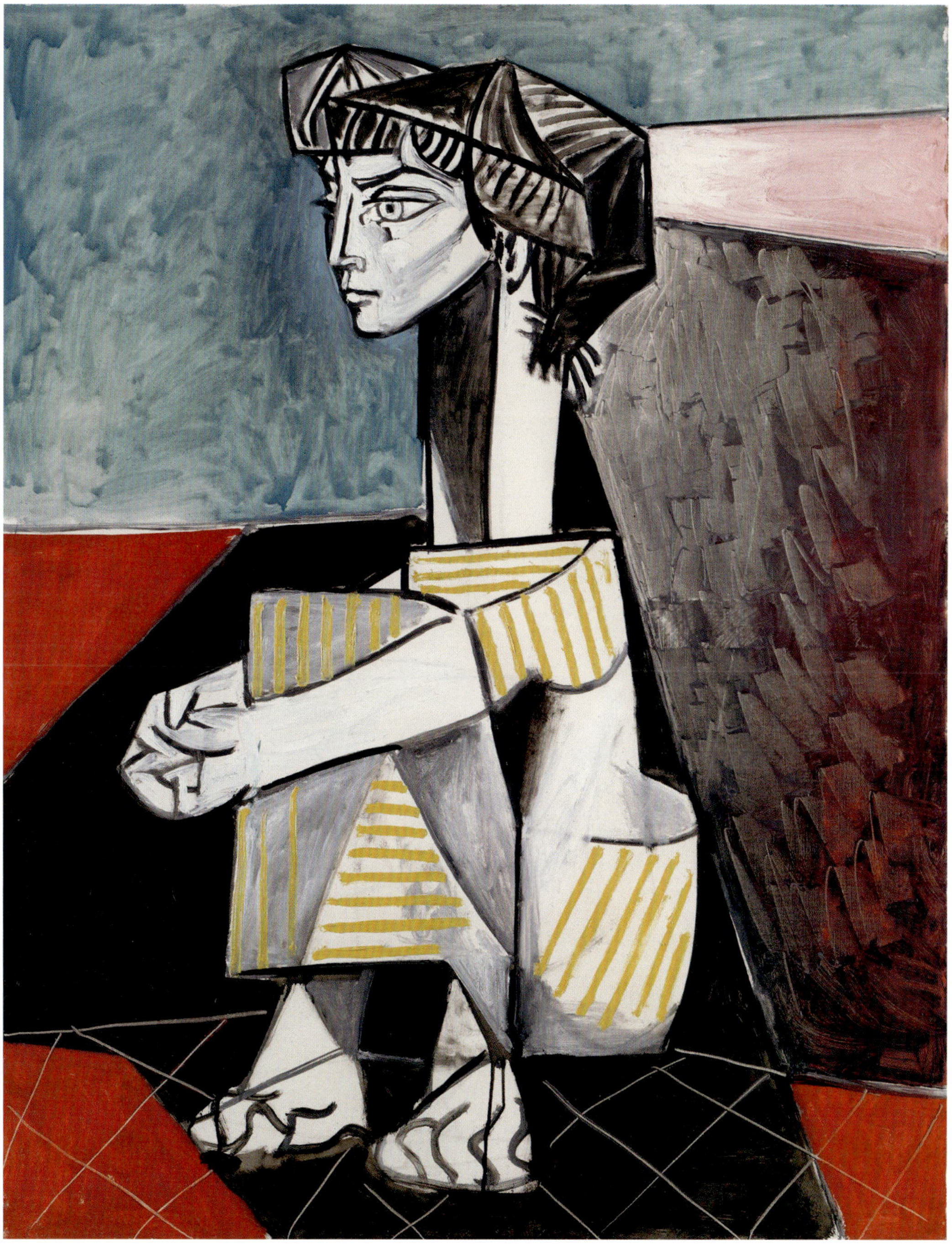

Jacqueline with Crossed Hands, June 3, 1954

1960
1972

"For me, a picture is the sum of destruction. I make a painting, and then destroy it."

Pablo Picasso, in Christian Zervos, "Conversations avec Picasso," *Cahiers d'art* (special edition, 1935)

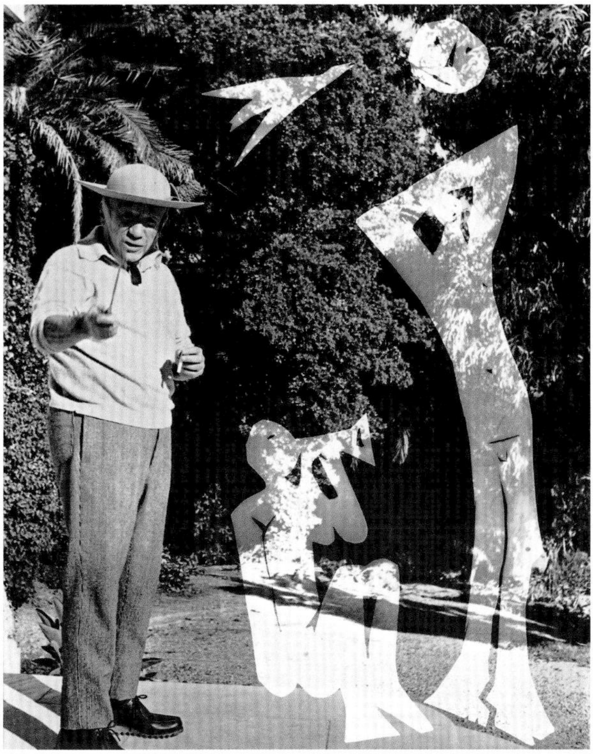

Picasso in his garden at La Californie with his cutouts superimposed, Cannes, 1961, by André Villers

For Picasso the 1950s and 1960s marked the time for a final revolution. In tribute to Henri Matisse, who had been his mentor, friend, and rival from 1905, and who died in autumn 1954, the artist embarked on an epic rereading of the history of painting. He summoned up the late artist in *L'Atelier de La Californie* (*The Studio at La Californie*, 1956), where, against a moresque backdrop, the blank areas of the canvas still quiver with the master's presence. With the cycle of variations on Velázquez's *Las Meninas*, on Manet's *Déjeuner sur l'herbe*, and on Delacroix's *Femmes d'Alger* (*Women of Algiers*), Picasso unfolded a radical interpretation of the masterpieces of painting. From variant to variant, in what emerges as a fully fledged artistic system, Picasso laid bare the bonds, transpositions, and ruptures by which these works are linked, and questioned his own position on the spiral of pictorial revolutions accomplished by modern art. The matadors with swords, the musicians with instruments, the gentlemen in hats and ruffs, the reclining nudes in drapes, and the hieratic portraits that henceforth begin to haunt his compositions all derive from pictures by Velázquez, Rembrandt, Goya or Titian, Delacroix, Ingres, and Manet. Their poses and dialogs, their embraces and conflicts all draw on the abundant saga of an iconographic tradition whose postures Picasso parodies and whose forms he subverts.

This reconfiguration of art finds more intimate echoes in his painted oeuvre. Portraying the woman who was to become the artist's last muse and his wife, the portrait of *Jacqueline aux mains croisées* (*Jacqueline with Crossed Hands*) of 1954 presents an enigmatic resemblance to the seated figure in Delacroix's *Femmes d'Alger*. In 1955, *Femme nue allongée* (*Reclining Nude Woman*), improvised under the eye of the camera during filming for Henri-Georges Clouzot's *Mystère Picasso* (*The Mystery of Picasso*), transformed Jacqueline into an odalisque made of multicolored wallpaper. Reverting once again to the studio techniques of cutout, folded, pinned, and stuck papers, Picasso then produced fragile models in paper or cardboard that transposed his pictorial researches into three dimensions. Simultaneously, collaborating with the young photographer André Villers, he pursued his photographic experimentation with cutouts and photograms (from 1954 to 1961), which appear in the book, *Diurnes* (1962), with a preface by Jacques Prévert. Encompassing drawing, découpage, folding, and photography, this circular process culminated in a sculptural reawakening epitomized by the folded metal works of the years 1957–62, in which masks, figures, nudes, and faces attained a markedly theoretical form. Painted white like his surrealist sculptures, these giant folding works are attempts to eliminate material and shift the emphasis onto the intricate shadows they cast. *Tête de femme* (*Head of a Woman*, 1957), *La Chaise* (*The Chair,* 1961), *Pierrot assis* (*Seated Pierrot*, 1961), *Femme au chapeau* (*Woman in a Hat*, 1961), and *Femme à l'enfant* (*Woman and Child*, 1961) allow one to appreciate the ambiguous interplay between the unfolding of a plane in space and its optical deformation in accordance with the nature and intensity of a light source. These ghostly white sculptures thus propagate a vast array of shadowy figures—impalpable and transitory.

In the paintings of the time too, flattened forms, sharp outlines, and cropped shapes generated, in positive or negative, the outlines of *Femmes à la toilette* (*Women in the Bathroom*, 1956), *Femme assise* (*Seated Woman*, 1963), and *Musicien* (*Musician*, 1972). These planar figures possess both the emblematic concision and the tragic character of tarot cards. Declining the forms of history painting in the present tense, while pursuing an urgent to-and-fro between painting and sculpture, Picasso continued to develop a critical stance and, up to the very last years, to learn from art. His creations express a tireless, eminently lyrical renewal of visual language. The garish colors and the vigorous brushwork that mark the figures in flows, squirts, and impastos, testify to his undimmed vehemence and vitality. Through painting, both the imminence of death, and his denial of it, are exorcised, parried, rejected.

Picasso conjured up a long line of his beloved masters in a series of self-portraits as an ascetic, a bullfighter, a mariner, or a Spanish grandee, complete with ruff and wig. In *Dimanche* (*Sunday*, 1971), he is flanked by Goya, El Greco, and Velázquez. Renoir is called forth in *Vieil homme assis* (*Seated Old Man*, 1971), painted from a photograph, showing the sick painter with a brush stuck into the bandages of his stumped hand. Executed shortly before his own death, *Le Jeune Peintre* (*The Young Painter*, 1972)—the paint scraped off in places around the burning eye-sockets—sports Van Gogh's straw hat. This last self-portrait encapsulates the freedom Picasso acquired, conquered, during a lifetime of struggle, thereby showing us that, in the end, painting had indeed "made him do what it wanted."

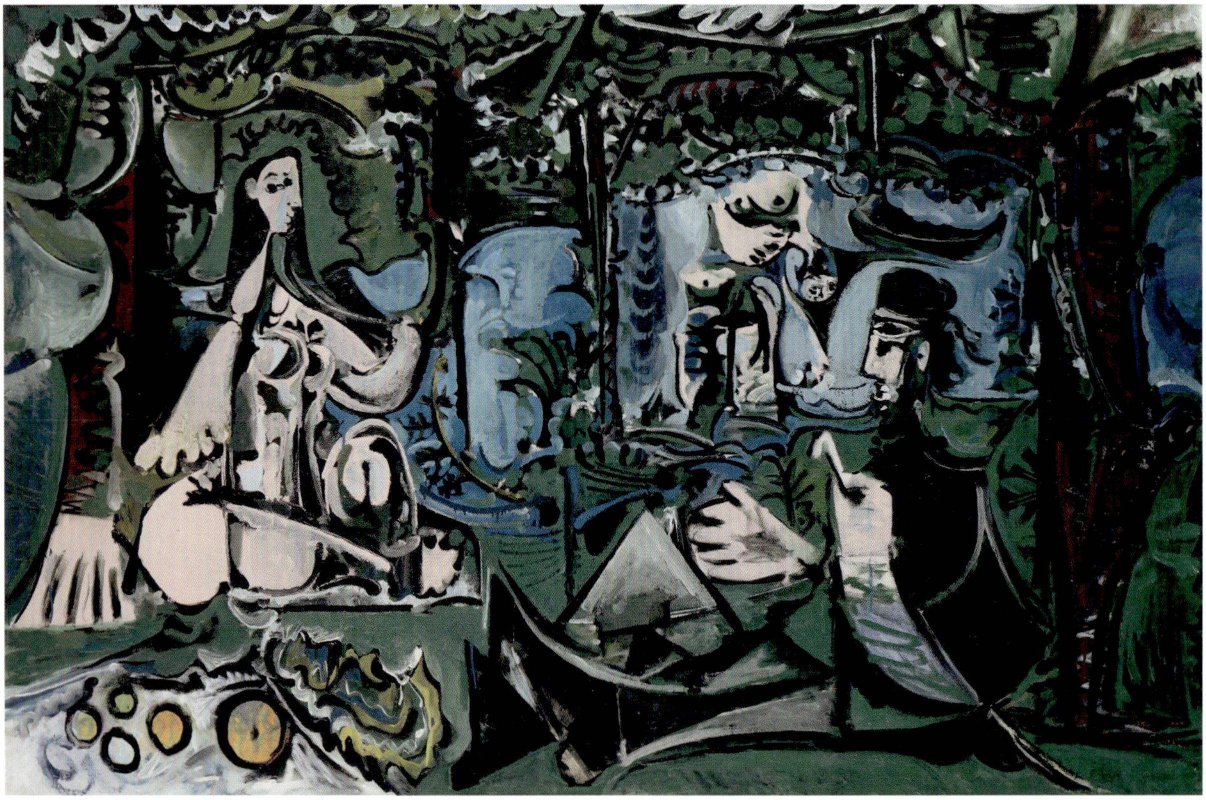

90 *Le Déjeuner sur l'Herbe after Manet*, March 3–August 20, 1960

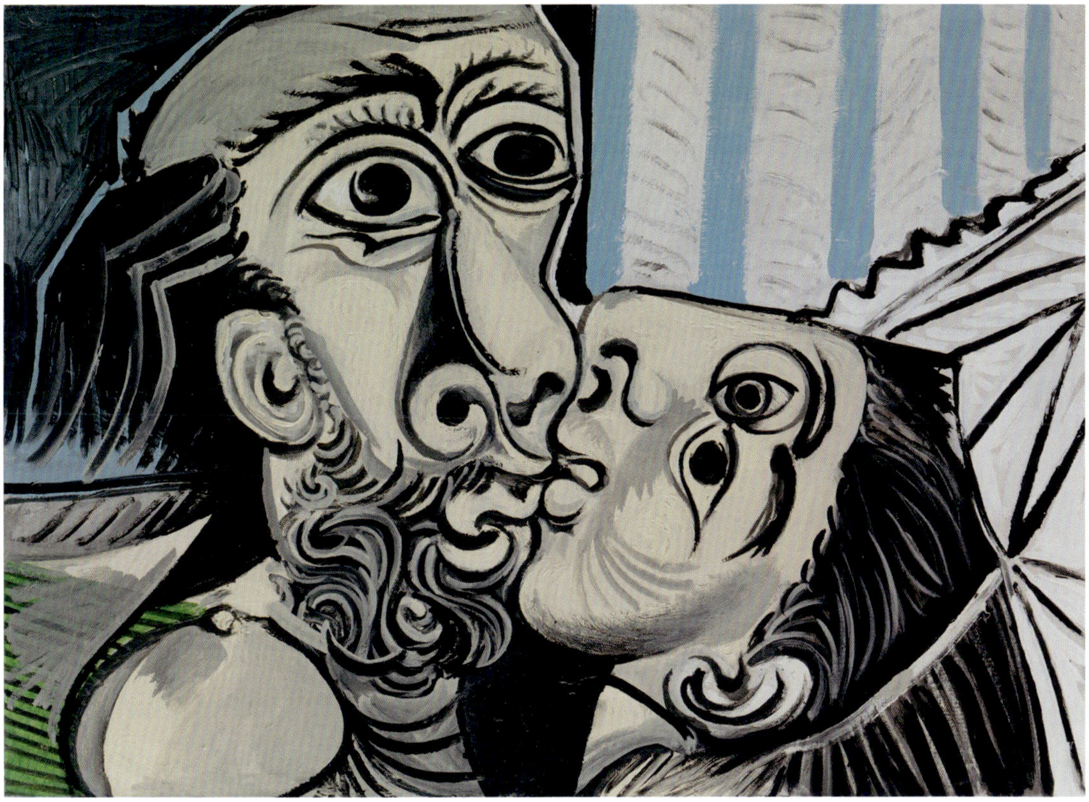

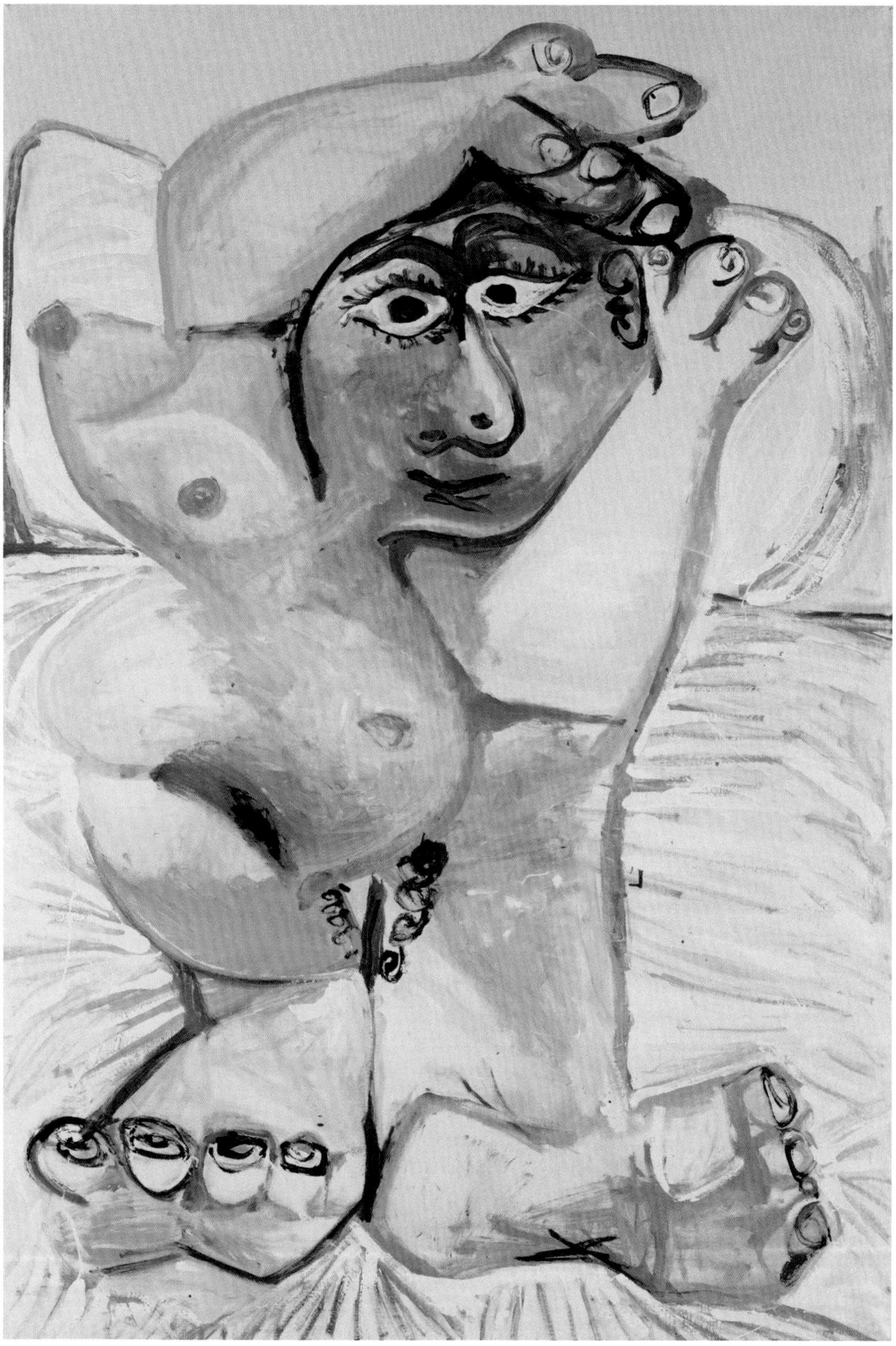

 Reclining Nude, June 14, 1967

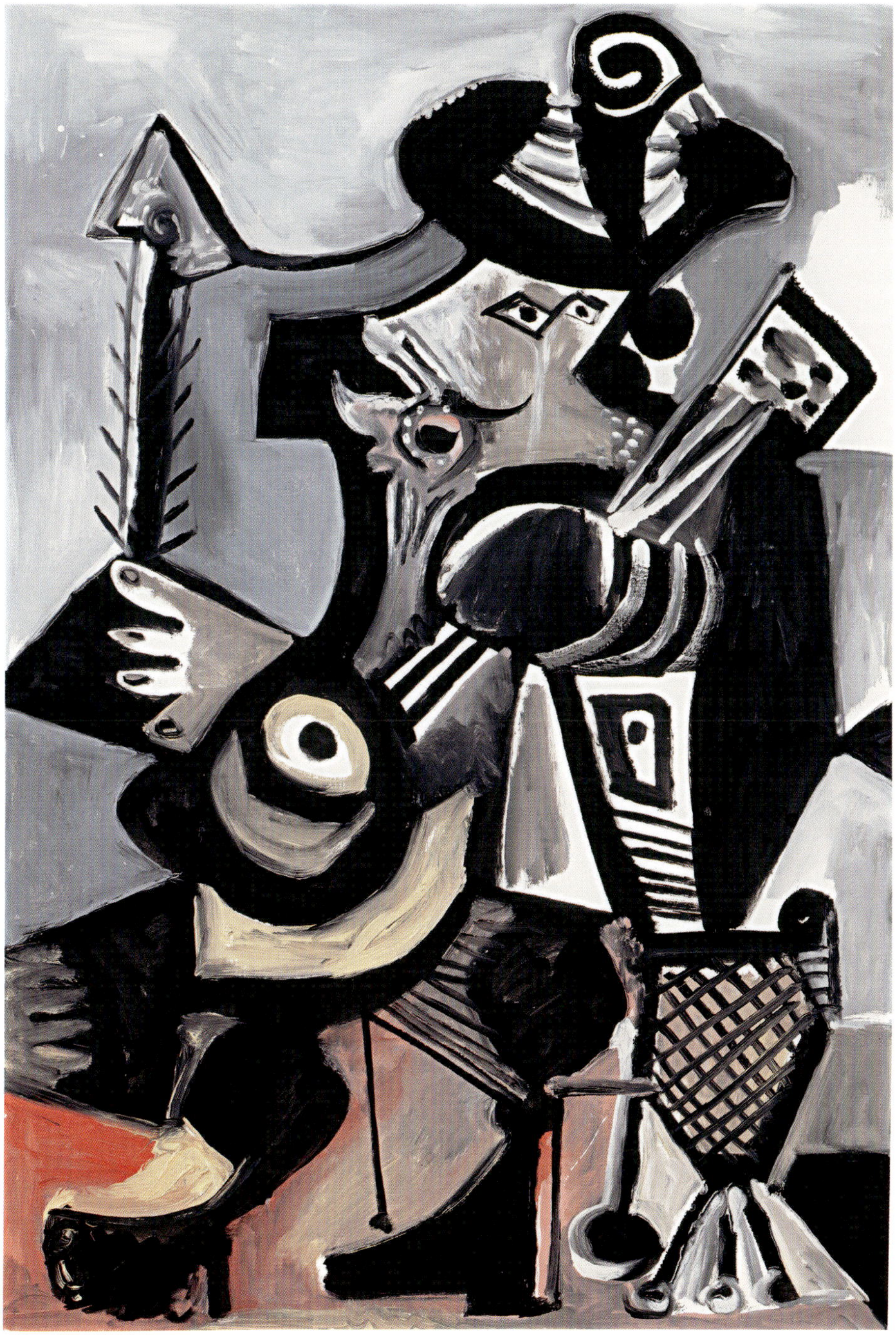

Musician, May 26, 1972

Chronology

1881

Pablo Picasso is born on October 25 in Malaga, son of Don José Ruiz Blasco (1838–1913) and of Doña Maria Picasso y Lopez (1855–1939).

1892–97

Aged just eleven Picasso begins his studies at the Fine Arts School in La Coruña, then at La Lonja in Barcelona and the Royal Academy of San Fernando, Madrid.

1899–1903

Exhibition of 150 drawings at Els Quatre Gats in Barcelona.
His picture *The Final Moments* is selected to represent Spain at the 1900 Paris World's Fair.
First visit to Paris.
Pedro Mañach introduces him to Berthe Weill and Ambroise Vollard.
His friend Carles Casagemas commits suicide in a Paris café.
Debut exhibition in Paris at the Vollard gallery in 1901.
Meets Max Jacob.
Berthe Weill shows early paintings from the Blue Period.

1904–5

Sets up his studio at the Bateau-Lavoir in Montmartre.
Meets a model, Fernande Olivier, who will become his partner, as well as writers and art critics, such as André Salmon, Guillaume Apollinaire, and Gertrude Stein.
Frequents the café Au Lapin Agile and the Cirque Medrano.
Onset of the Rose Period.
Travels to the Netherlands.
Meets Henri Matisse.

1906–8

Studies Iberian sculpture in the Louvre.
Sojourn in Gósol.
Embarks on a large-scale composition in winter 1906, *Les Demoiselles d'Avignon*, which he reworks following a visit to the ethnography museum at the Trocadéro in June 1907.
Becomes friends with the Douanier Rousseau and Georges Braque.
Meets art collector Sergei Shchukin.

1909–12

Journey to Horta de Ebro, where he develops a radical variant of early "Cézannian cubism."
Backed by the Steins, Vollard, and Kahnweiler, he sets up his studio in a new locale on boulevard de Clichy.
Participates in seminal modern art exhibitions such as *Manet and the Post-Impressionists* in London and the 22nd Berlin Secession.
Vollard dedicates a final exhibition in Paris to Picasso.
Picasso exhibition at the 291 gallery, New York.
Liaison with Eva Gouel (Marcelle Humbert).
Takes part in 1912 in the Jack of Diamonds show in Moscow, the Blaue Reiter in Munich, the Berlin Secession, the *Internationale Kunst-Ausstellung des Sonderbundes Westdeutscher Kunstfreunde und Künstler* in Cologne, and in the *Second Post-Impressionist Exhibition* in London.
Picasso composes the first "collage," *Still Life with Cane Chair*.
Takes on a new studio at 242, boulevard Raspail, and signs a three-year contract with Kahnweiler.
Du cubisme by Albert Gleizes and Jean Metzinger.

1913–14

Picasso participates in the *Die Neue Kunst* exhibition in Vienna, the Neue Kunstsalon in Munich, the *International Exhibition of Modern Art* at the Armory Show, New York, and the *Post-Impressionist and Futurist Exhibition*, London.
First Picasso retrospective in Germany at Heinrich Thannhauser's Moderne Galerie, Munich.
Méditations esthétiques. Les peintres cubistes by Apollinaire.
Picasso's father dies on May 3, 1913.
With Eva, Picasso sets up a new studio at 5 bis, rue Schoelcher in summer 1913.
Sold at auction in March 1914 as part of the Peau de l'Ours collection, *The Family of Acrobats* (1905) fetches ten times its initial price.
Cubistes, futuristes, passéistes. Essai sur la jeune peinture et la jeune sculpture by Gustave Coquiot.
Picasso takes part in the Sommerschau 1914 exhibition, Munich.
Germany declares war on France.
Picasso stays on in Avignon until late November.
Picasso-Braque exhibition at the 291 gallery, New York.

1915–16

Braque is seriously wounded.
Eva dies.
Apollinaire is wounded and has to be trepanned.
Les Demoiselles d'Avignon is unveiled at *L'Art moderne en France* (the Salon d'Antin).
Picasso moves to Montrouge.
Becoming friends with Erik Satie, he participates in Jean Cocteau's exhibition *Lyre et Palette*.

1917–20

Stays in Rome, Naples, and Pompeii with the troupe of the Ballets Russes working on *Parade*.
Premiere of *Parade* (script by Jean Cocteau, music by Erik Satie, choreography by Léonide Massine, curtain, sets, and costumes by Picasso, program by Guillaume Apollinaire) at the Théâtre du Châtelet.
Matisse-Picasso exhibition at Galerie Paul Guillaume.
July 12, 1918, Picasso weds Olga Khokhlova at the Russian church on rue Daru.
His witnesses are Jacob, Apollinaire, and Cocteau.
Honeymoon in Biarritz, in Eugenia Errazuriz's house where he meets art dealers Paul Rosenberg and Georges Wildenstein, and banker Joseph Essel, who establish a consortium to promote his work.
Joins dealer Paul Rosenberg.
Death of Guillaume Apollinaire on November 9, 1918.
Picasso moves to 23, rue La Boétie.
Premiere in summer 1919 of *The Three-Cornered Hat*, a ballet by Diaghilev (after Pedro de Alarcón, choreography by Léonide Massine, sets and curtain by Picasso, and music by Manuel de Falla) at the Alhambra Theatre, London.
Paul Rosenberg shows drawings and paintings by Picasso.
Daniel-Henry Kahnweiler publishes his book *Der Weg zum Kubismus* (*The Rise of Cubism*).
In May 1920, first performance of *Pulcinella* at the Paris Opera (music by Igor Stravinsky after Pergolesi, choreography by Léonide Massine, sets and costumes by Picasso).

1921–23

A committee of artists appoints Picasso to create a monument for Apollinaire's tomb in the Père-Lachaise cemetery.
Birth of Picasso and Olga's son, Paul, on February 4, 1921.
Publication of the first monograph devoted to Picasso by Maurice Raynal.
Première of *Cuadro Flamenco* at the Théâtre de la Gaîté-Lyrique, Paris (traditional music adapted by Manuel de Falla, choreography by Léonide Massine, sets and costumes by Picasso).
Sale of Wilhelm Uhde's

collection confiscated in 1914 (sixteen Picassos).
Four sales at the Hôtel Drouot between June 1921 and May 1923 of property sequestered from Kahnweiler's gallery in 1914 (ninety-six works by Picasso are sold).
Picasso show at Galerie Paul Rosenberg.
Meets Comte Étienne de Beaumont and the American painter Gerald Murphy.
Affair with Sarah Murphy.
Picasso Recent Works at Wildenstein Gallery, New York; *Picasso* at the Art Institute of Chicago.

1924–26

Jacques Doucet buys *Les Demoiselles d'Avignon.*
Exhibits regularly at Galerie Paul Rosenberg.
Premiere of the ballet *Mercure* at the Théâtre de la Cigale staged by Comte Étienne de Beaumont (curtain, scenery, and costumes by Picasso, music by Erik Satie, and choreography by Léonide Massine).
Picasso stays in Monte-Carlo with Olga and Paul during the Ballets Russes' season.
Paints *La Danse* (*The Dance*).

1927–30

Picasso meets Marie-Thérèse Walter (1907–1977), then seventeen.
Paul Rosenberg exhibits one hundred drawings by Picasso.
Constructs metal models of his *Monument to Guillaume Apollinaire* in Julio González's workshop.
Picasso et la tradition française: notes sur la peinture actuelle by Wilhelm Uhde.
Picasso buys the Château de Boisgeloup, near Gisors, where he sets up a sculpture workshop.
Receives the Carnegie Prize for *Portrait of Olga in Profile.*

1931–36

At Boisgeloup Picasso produces a series of large busts and heads in plaster.
Quelques œuvres importantes de Picasso at Galerie Paul Rosenberg.
Les Métamorphoses d'Ovide illustrated with thirty etchings by Picasso.
Balzac's *Le Chef-d'Œuvre inconnu*, with thirteen etchings by Picasso.
Picasso retrospective at Georges Petit's gallery in Paris and then at the Kunsthaus, Zurich.
Picasso peintre graveur, catalogue illustré de l'œuvre gravé et lithographié 1899–1931 by Bernhard Geiser.
Picasso and His Friends first published in French by Fernande Olivier.
Papiers collés de Picasso, 1912–1914 at the Galerie Pierre, with a text by Tristan Tzara.
Lysistrata after Aristophanes, with forty prints by Picasso.
Picasso stops painting until February 1936 and begins to write poetry seriously.
Picasso and Olga separate but do not divorce.
Jaime Sabartés becomes Picasso's secretary.
Birth of a daughter to Marie-Thérèse and Picasso, Maria de la Concepción, known as Maya.
The Spanish Popular Front wins the elections.
Picasso retrospective in Barcelona organized by the ADLAN group.
Exposition d'œuvres récentes de Picasso at Galerie Paul Rosenberg.
The Popular Front wins the French elections.
Picasso takes part in the surrealist events *Exposition surréaliste d'objets* at Charles Ratton's gallery, *The Second International Surrealist Exhibition* at the New Burlington Galleries, London, and *Fantastic Art, Dada and Surrealism* at the Museum of Modern Art, New York.
Contributes to the exhibition of the Maison de la Culture at the Théâtre de l'Alhambra organized by Louis Aragon, and creates the curtain for Romain Rolland's play *Le 14 Juillet.*
Spanish Civil War.
Named honorary director of the Prado by the Spanish Republic.

1937–39

Picasso rents a studio on rue des Grands-Augustins, Paris.
Dream and Lie of Franco series.
Guernica is bombed.
The Spanish pavilion at the Exposition Internationale des Arts et Techniques, Paris, opens, unveiling the large-scale composition, *Guernica.*
First exhibition of "degenerate art" in Munich.
Guernica exhibition in London, Leeds, and Liverpool under the auspices of the National Joint Committee for Spanish Relief. It will also be presented in New York, Los Angeles, Chicago, and San Francisco.
Death of Picasso's mother in Barcelona.
125 works of "degenerate art" (including four Picassos) auctioned off at the Galerie Fischer, Lucerne.
Death of Ambroise Vollard.
Picasso retreats to Royan.
Germany invades Poland. Great Britain and France declare war on Germany.
Brassaï carries out a reportage on Picasso for *Life* magazine on the occasion of an exhibition at the Museum of Modern Art, New York, entitled *Picasso: Forty Years of His Art.*

1940–45

Picasso lives between Royan and Paris. With Franco threatening to request his extradition he asks for French nationality, but is rejected.
Remains in Paris throughout the Occupation.
Buffon's *Histoire naturelle* illustrated by Picasso.
Meets the 22-year-old painter, Françoise Gilot.
Max Jacob is sent to the concentration camp at Drancy, where he dies on March 5, 1944.
The communist newspaper *L'Humanité* proclaims Picasso's adhesion to the French Communist Party (PCF).
The Salon d'Automne de la Libération hosts a Picasso retrospective (seventy-four paintings and five sculptures).
Performance at the Leiris's home of Picasso's play *Le Désir attrapé par la queue*, directed by Albert Camus.
Exhibitions *Picasso Libre* at the Galerie Louis Carré and *Picasso and Matisse* at the Victoria and Albert Museum, London.

1946–49

Louis Carré shows nineteen paintings by Picasso.
Alfred H. Barr publishes *Picasso: Forty Years of His Art.*
Picasso spends the summer at the Château Grimaldi, Antibes.
Death of Nusch Éluard.
Picasso: portraits et souvenirs by Jaime Sabartés.
Picasso donates ten canvases to the Musée National d'Art Moderne, Paris.
Claude, Françoise Gilot's first child, is born in 1947.
Official opening of a Picasso room in the museum at Antibes.
Guernica: Pablo Picasso by Juan Larrea.
Filmmaker Paul Haesaerts makes *Visite à Picasso.*
Picasso shows at the Venice Biennale.
Moves with Françoise to La Galloise, Vallauris.
Takes part in the World Congress of Intellectuals for Peace in Wroclaw, Poland, and joins the call to free Pablo Neruda.
Le Chant des morts by Pierre Reverdy (125 lithographs by Picasso).
Vingt poèmes by Luis de Góngora (forty-one plates by Picasso).
Sculptures de Picasso by Daniel-Henry Kahnweiler, with photographs by Brassaï and Dora Maar.
Aragon chooses Picasso's lithograph *The Dove* for the poster for the Peace Congress.
Birth of Paloma, Françoise Gilot and Picasso's second child.
The Peace Congress opens at the Salle Pleyel, Paris.
Picasso acquires a studio at Le Fournas, Vallauris.
Carmen by Prosper Mérimée (thirty-eight plates by Picasso).
L'Humanité publishes a drawing by Picasso entitled *Your very good health, Stalin!*, sparking lively debate within the PCF.

1950–53

Corps perdu by Aimé Césaire (etchings by Picasso).
Inauguration of *Man with a Sheep* on the place du Marché, Vallauris.
Picasso is present at the Second Peace Conference, in Sheffield, Great Britain.

Receives the Lenin Peace Prize. Paints *Massacre in Korea,* shown at the Salon de Mai in 1951.
Large-scale Picasso retrospective in Tokyo and Osaka.
Embarks on a pair of monumental panels, *War* and *Peace*, to decorate a fourteenth-century chapel in Vallauris.
Death of Paul Éluard.
Finishes his play, *Les Quatre Petites Filles.*
Draws a *Portrait of Stalin* for *Les Lettres françaises*, vehemently attacked by the Central Committee of the PCF.
Françoise Gilot leaves Picasso and moves to Paris with their children.
Director Luciano Emmer shoots the film *Picasso.*
Picasso retrospectives at the Galleria Nazionale d'Arte Moderna, Rome, then at the Palazzo Reale, Milan, the Museu de Arte Moderna, São Paulo, and the Musée des Beaux-Arts, Lyon.
Separates from Geneviève Laporte.
Sabartés donates his personal collection to the city of Barcelona.

1954–59

La Guerre et la Paix by Claude Roy, illustrated by Picasso.
Exhibition of Picasso prints at the Kunsthaus, Zurich, accompanied by a catalogue raisonné by Bernhard Geiser and Hans Bolliger.
Meets Jacqueline Roque at the Galerie Madoura.
Picasso: deux périodes, 1900–1914, 1950–1954 at the Maison de la Pensée Française includes works from the Shchukin collection never previously shown outside Soviet museums.
Death of Henri Matisse on November 3, 1954.
On February 11, 1955, Olga Picasso dies in Cannes.
Retrospective *Picasso: Paintings, 1900–1955* at the Musée des Arts Décoratifs, Paris, before traveling to Munich, Cologne, and Hamburg.
Picasso purchases the villa La Californie in Cannes.
Attends bullfights in Arles and Nîmes, forging a friendship with the famous torero, Luis Miguel Dominguín.
Henri-Georges Clouzot's *Le Mystère Picasso* is presented at the Cannes Film Festival in 1956.
The photographer David Douglas Duncan takes pictures of Picasso's daily life (*The Private World of Pablo Picasso,* 1958).
First Picasso exhibition in Barcelona, at the Sala Gaspar.
Ilya Ehrenburg organizes a Picasso exhibition at the Pushkin Museum in Moscow and the Hermitage in Leningrad comprising works from Russian collections and from the artist's own collection.
Picasso: 75th Anniversary Exhibition, at the Museum of Modern Art, New York, then in Chicago and Philadelphia.
A show of drawings, gouaches, and watercolors from 1898 to 1957 at the Musée Réattu, Arles, with a catalog by Douglas Cooper, and of 150 ceramic pieces at the Maison de la Pensée Française.
1958 sees the inauguration of the vast *Fall of Icarus* in the lobby of UNESCO in Paris.
Picasso purchases the Château de Vauvenargues in the foothills of the Montagne Sainte-Victoire.
The bronze *Head* of Dora Maar (1941) is erected on the square behind the Church of Saint-Germain-des-Prés.
The chapel at Vallauris, decorated with panels of *War* and *Peace,* opens.
La Tauromaquía o arte de torear by José Delgado, illustrated by Picasso.
Picasso acts in Jean Cocteau's film *Testament d'Orphée.*

1960–64

Picasso. Retrospective 1895–1959 at the Tate Gallery, London; *Picasso, pinturas, 30 cuadros inéditos 1917–1960*, at the Sala Gaspar, Barcelona; *Bonne Fête Monsieur Picasso from Southern California Collectors*, at the UCLA Art Gallery, Los Angeles; *Peintures de Vauvenargues (1959–1961)* in Louise Leiris's gallery; *Picasso: An American Tribute* at the Cordier Warren Gallery, New York; *80th Birthday Exhibition: The Museum Collection, Present and Future* at the Museum of Modern Art, New York.
Picasso weds Jacqueline Roque in Vallauris in 1961.
Moves into the *mas* Notre-Dame-de-Vie, in Mougins.
David Douglas Duncan publishes *Picasso's Picassos.*
Picasso receives the Lenin Peace Prize for the second time.
Works on a project for scenery for the ballet *Icare,* staged at the Paris Opera by Serge Lifar.
The Museu Picasso opens in Barcelona.
Death of Georges Braque on August 31.
Death of Jean Cocteau on October 11.
Picasso begins a collaboration with printmakers Aldo and Piero Crommelynck, who set up a studio in Mougins.
Retrospectives *Picasso and Man* at the Art Gallery, Toronto; *Works from 1899 to 1963* at the National Museum of Modern Art, Tokyo, Kyoto, and Nagoya.
Brassaï's *Conversations with Picasso* is published in French.

1965–73

Françoise Gilot's *Life with Picasso* first published in French.
Picasso undergoes an operation at the American Hospital, Neuilly; last sojourn in Paris.
The monumental *Déjeuner sur l'herbe after Manet* is installed in the park of the Moderna Museet, Stockholm.
Suite of *60 gravures.*
Death of André Breton on September 28.
Hommage à Picasso at the Grand Palais and the Petit Palais, Paris.
Refuses to accept the Légion d'Honneur in 1967.
Picasso: Sculptures, Ceramics, Graphic Work, at the Tate Gallery, London, and then the Museum of Modern Art, New York.
Inauguration of the large welded steel *Head* erected at the Civic Art Center in Chicago.
Picasso donates the series of *Las Meninas* (fifty-eight canvases) and a portrait of Sabartés to the Museu Picasso, Barcelona.
Executes the sequence of *347 gravures.*
A monumental bust of *Sylvette* is set up in a courtyard in New York University.
Pablo Picasso. Catalogue de l'œuvre gravé et lithographié, vol. 1, by Georges Bloch; *Picasso peintre graveur, catalogue illustré de l'œuvre gravé et lithographié*, vol. 2, by Bernhard Geiser.
Picasso's play *Les Quatre Petites Filles* is published.
El Entierro del Conde de Orgaz, with a text and illustrations by Picasso, and a prologue by Rafael Alberti.
In 1970, donates youthful works left in Spain to the Museu Picasso, Barcelona.
Picasso 1969–1970 exhibition (167 paintings and 45 drawings) at the Palais des Papes, Avignon, causes a public scandal.
The Bateau-Lavoir burns down.
Death of Christian Zervos on September 12.
194 Dessins (1969–1971) at Louise Leiris's gallery.
Gift by Picasso of fifty-seven drawings to the Musée Réattu, Arles.
On the occasion of the artist's ninetieth birthday, works from French public collections are shown in the Grande Galerie of the Louvre.
La Célestine by Fernando de Rojas (1499), illustrated with seventy etchings by Picasso.
Donates the sheet-metal *Guitar* of 1912 to William Rubin for the Museum of Modern Art, New York.
Continues to paint up until August 18, 1972.
Louise Leiris's gallery shows 172 drawings in black and white and color, as well as 156 recent prints.
April 8, 1973: Picasso dies in the *mas* Notre-Dame-de-Vie in Mougins.
He is buried on April 10 in the garden of the château at Vauvenargues.
Jacqueline Picasso has *Woman with Vase,* a bronze of 1933, set up on his tombstone.
The exhibition *Pablo Picasso, 1970–1972* is held in the Palais des Papes, Avignon, with a preface by René Char.